How to Have a Happy Marriage

How to Have a Happy Marriage

A Step-by-Step Guide to an Enriched Relationship

David and Vera Mace

Abingdon Press ○ Nashville

HOW TO HAVE A HAPPY MARRIAGE
A Step-by-Step Guide to an Enriched Relationship

Copyright © 1977 by Abingdon

This book is printed on recycled acid-free paper

Library of Congress Cataloging in Publication Data
MACE, DAVID ROBERT.
How to have a happy marriage.
Bibliography: p.
1. Marriage. 2. Interpersonal relations. I. Mace, Vera, joint author. II. Title.
HQ734.M1842   301.42′7   77-7575

ISBN 0-687-17832-0
Formerly published under ISBN 0-687-17830-4 and ISBN 0-687-17831-2

Poem "Epithalamium" by Jan Struther on p. 43 is reprinted by permission of Curtis Brown, Ltd. Copyright © 1941, 1969 by Jan Struther.

96 97 98 99 00 01 02 03 04 — 20 19 18 17 16 15

MANUFACTURED IN THE UNITED STATES OF AMERICA

Preface

The purpose of this book will be clear from the title and from a glance at the contents page. There *are* other books that try to help married couples to improve their relationship. In what ways is this one different?

First, as the authors, we can claim a long and continuous association with this field. For more than forty years, we have worked to develop marriage counseling all over the world, and we have ourselves counseled with thousands of couples in trouble. In addition, during the past fourteen years, we have been pioneers in the marriage enrichment movement, leading weekend retreats for couples who have wanted to improve their relationships. This extensive experience of seeing marriages from the inside has given us a very clear picture of what happens when a marriage doesn't succeed, and of what can be done to prevent such a failure.

Second, during our forty years of marriage counseling, we have been working continually on our own relationship; so what we talk about in this book is not just theory. It has all worked for us personally, and we therefore pass it on to others with confidence that it can work for them too.

Third, we have structured the book so that it gives specific guidance to any couple who will make a contract to work with us. It isn't just a book for reading. It is very definitely a *work book,* to be used by the couple in actually examining and restructuring their relationship. We are even prepared to guarantee that any normal couple can improve their relationship if they will faithfully follow our directions.

Fourth, the book uses direct, person-to-person conversations between the reader couple and us, using this approach as far as is possible through the medium of the printed page. We have tried to make the book very easy to read, using clear, nontechnical language and keeping the chapters short. We have not hesitated to make use of that tried and tested technique of good teaching—repetition for the sake of emphasis. What we ask is that the reader couple contract with us for six weeks of very specific working on their marriage, and we give them detailed instructions about what to do.

Despite our detailed and practical approach, however, this book should not be viewed as a substitute for either personal or marriage counseling. There are people who need—and must have—the kind of help that can only be provided by face-to-face interviews with a qualified therapist. We try in the book to encourage couples of this kind to find the professional help they need.

We have written this book primarily as a way of reaching out to the individual couple and of offering the kind of help we have been giving in face-to-face work with couples for forty years—but the book is also designed to be used in other ways. A group of couples could very profitably work through it together, meeting each week for six weeks to report their progress to one another. A counselor could arrange for a couple, or a group of couples, to work through the book, reporting progress in weekly interviews. A pastor could use it to enable couples to do basic work on their marriages, giving them supplementary personal guidance, and in this way save himself a great deal of time. Other professionals, such as physicians, social workers, and lawyers, could likewise give or lend the book to married couples seeking their help. Finally, the book might be a welcome gift from a relative or friend to a couple about to marry or to remarry.

Our hope is that educators will also make use of our book, for it demonstrates the exciting new possibilities of what is beginning to be called experiential education—the process of "learning by doing."

This book, in short, represents a new venture in a new field. At a time when many professionals are overwhelmed with appeals for help from people whose marriages are in trouble, it represents an attempt to guide couples in the process of developing their own resources in order to help themselves. If, as we hope, the book is widely used, we would expect to revise and update later editions on the basis of experience gained. We would therefore welcome suggestions from people who use it—either the couples themselves or professionals. We have included, at the end of the book, a questionnaire for this purpose.

We express our gratitude to many people—too numerous to mention individually—who have made it possible for us to write this book. The one name we do want to record is that of Kay Evans, who, from dictation, typed an almost faultless manuscript in record time.

David and Vera Mace

Contents

PART I. A Growth Plan for Your Marriage..........**11**

   1. The Couple Who Made It 13

   2. Setting the Stage 18

   3. What We Offer You 23

   4. The Program Outlined 30

PART II. An Honest Look at Your Relationship **37**

   5. How Marriages Can Grow 39

   6. Marital Growth in Our Changing Culture 44

   7. What's Your Marriage Potential?.............50

   8. Getting to Work—Together 57

   9. Work Unit for First and Second Weeks 62

PART III. Learning to Communicate Effectively ... **69**

   10. Can You Hear Me, Darling? 71

   11. Getting in Touch with Each Other 77

   12. What Style Are You In? 83

   13. Work Units for Third
        and Fourth Weeks.......................89

PART IV. Resolving Conflicts Creatively **97**

    14. Never Waste a Good Conflict 99

    15. How to Deal with Anger 108

    16. Settling Disagreements by Negotiation 116

    17. Work Units for Fifth
        and Sixth Weeks 124

PART V. Where Do We Go from Here? **131**

    18. Looking Back and Looking Forward 133

    19. Some Secondary Areas of
        Marital Adjustment 139

    20. Working with a Marriage Counselor 146

    21. Joining a Couples' Growth Group 152

    22. Getting into the Marriage
        Enrichment Movement 158

APPENDICES **163**

    A. Summary of Work Units 163

    B. Some Good Books for Further Reading 165

    C. National Marriage Enrichment
        Organizations in North America 169

    D. More About the Maces 171

    E. Evaluation Form 173

PART I
A Growth Plan for Your Marriage

1
The Couple Who Made It

We want to tell you about Tom and Sue. Those are not their real names, but they are very real people. We know them and love them. We have been guests in their home and have heard their full story. To some, it will sound fantastic. To us, it is very moving and exciting.

After some years of marriage, Tom and Sue confronted the usual conflicts, struggled with the usual misunderstandings, and fell victim to the usual pressures. They were well on their way to arriving at the usual conclusion—"Marriage is overrated. All this romantic stuff is OK for fairy tales and old-time novels, but it just doesn't work in real life." They were about to cut their losses, settle down to dull mediocrity, and try to make the best of it for the sake of their two children.

Then, something happened. A streak of obstinacy appeared in them both. They found themselves unwilling to follow the dull, dreary, conventional road. Had their dreams of a warm, deep, tender, loving relationship been given them only to mock them? During ecstatic moments, and in peak experiences, they had tasted something different. They knew that life couldn't be lived on cloud nine, but deep down they had a persistent "gut feeling" that two married people *could* enjoy a rich, rewarding relationship; and they felt that if this were possible, they weren't going to be cheated out of it.

So Tom and Sue got into some long, earnest talks about what their marriage could mean to them. They saw it as a partnership in mutual growth—a way to help and encourage each other to become, over the years, the persons they were capable of becoming. They saw it as an unfailing source of mutual support, of emotional security, of creative loving; as a stimulus to keep on making life meaningful and purposeful; as a pilgrimage through the life-span undertaken together. They saw themselves in a warm and caring comradeship that could provide for their children a secure place for growing and learning and becoming. They saw themselves as a unified team reaching out to other married couples, offering out of their own experience a message of hope, reaffirming their own joy and fulfillment by sharing it with the people around them.

This was their dream. But was it possible? And if so, how could they make it come true?

Tom was a businessman who held a position of high responsibility in his firm. Sue was a homemaker and mother, living in a suburban community, who kept busy with all kinds of social activities among friends and neighbors, was devoted to her children, and was active in the church. The pressures on both of them were heavy—the telephone rang at all hours, friends dropped by to visit, social institutions and obligations pulled them in all directions. Tom brought work home on the weekends and took business trips out of town. Getting time alone together—time to look deep into themselves and to share deeply with one another—seemed so difficult that Tom and Sue felt constantly frustrated. It looked like a hopeless struggle against impossible odds.

And yet they knew that time alone together was what they desperately needed. Was there any way out?

One day, they made a startling decision.

Tom and Sue reached the conclusion that their marriage was

14

the most valuable thing they had—more important than Tom's career, more important than making money, more important than the children's educations, more important than their social obligations. They therefore decided that, for a time, they would give their marriage top priority. Whatever seemed best for the healthy development of their relationship would be put first, and nothing else would be allowed to stand in the way.

The decision was to take a whole year off—for the express purpose of working on their marriage! During that year, they would leave no stone unturned that might help them to achieve their goal. They would learn all they could, do whatever was needful, seek whatever help might be available. Everything else would be put aside for the achievement of this supreme and all-important goal.

So Tom told his boss, and his business colleagues, that they would have to manage without his services for a year. He might have lost his job, but he didn't—he's back at it today. Sue arranged to rent their home. And one day they set off, with the children and a good deal of baggage, on the adventure of their lives.

They began their quest by learning all that they could about marriage. They read books, attended conferences, took part in experiential workshops, sought out people who seemed to know the answers. Gradually, however, they became increasingly aware that while all this information was helpful, nobody outside their relationship could really do for them what was necessary. At home, time alone together had been their greatest need. And now, time alone together became, more and more convincingly, the means of achieving their goal.

At this point they made another dramatic decision. They and the children packed up and went to live on a remote island in the Mediterranean. In a setting of serene peace, under sunny skies and surrounded by the glittering sea, Tom and Sue looked deeply into their minds and hearts and sought understanding. Living simply and ignoring the calendar, they opened up their inner selves progressively to each other—a process sometimes exhilarating, often painful, but always healing. As they put it, "Before, we would get started on sharing some area of our lives. Then we had to break off and do something else. Nothing between us ever got finished. Now, there was no interruption and no excuse. We had the opportunity, and the necessity, to share completely all our thoughts, feelings, and needs."

So the year passed, and the time came to return home. Tom went back to his job. Sue took up again her tasks as homemaker, her life with friends and neighbors. The children went back to school. Soon husband and wife had settled into the old routines. Externally, everything was just the same as before. But internally, nothing was the same. Tom and Sue were different people. Their marriage was tinglingly alive. Their family life was radiantly happy.

We can bear personal testimony to this. For over a week after their return, we lived with them in their home. Their relationship to each other, and to their children, created a pervasive atmosphere of love and joy and peace. This, we said to each other, is a truly happy home—family life as it ought to be and can be, but alas, seldom is.

The joy that Tom and Sue have found in each other is something they cannot keep to themselves. They are actively engaged in the marriage enrichment movement. They are training to be marriage counselors. They are working for better marriages—having begun with their own.

We want to be very careful in explaining why we have told this story. We don't want to suggest that the only way a couple can get their marriage really going is to take a year off. For some, this could end in disaster. We don't want to suggest that without a course of intensive study, followed by a sojourn on a remote island, you can't really hope to get your relationship functioning. Tom and Sue would be the first to say that their way of dealing with their situation, while right for them, wouldn't necessarily be appropriate for others.

What we are trying to communicate, through the telling of this story, is a clear and simple message. It is that any couple who want to have a happy, loving relationship now have at their disposal considerable resources that just didn't exist before; moreover, if they will devote time, effort, and perseverance to the task, they can move a long way, possibly most of the way, toward achieving their goal.

An earlier book of ours was entitled *We Can Have Better Marriages—If We Really Want Them*. In that book, we tried to support convincingly the statement in the title—to provide evidence that this really *is* so. But when we wrote that book, we knew that one day we would have to follow it up with another—a book that would try, in very practical, down-to-earth terms, to show a couple exactly *how* this could be done. Your approach may turn out to be very different from that of Tom and Sue's. But we want to hold up Tom and Sue for your encouragement—as a couple who saw clearly how vital it was for them to have a really creative marriage, and who then found their own special way to achieve it.

Whatever way you choose, there are certain facts you will need to know and certain steps you will need to take. We ourselves, a married couple who have now been working on our relationship for forty-four years and still are working on it, will try to share with you the necessary facts—and guide you in taking the necessary steps—to get started. But, as Tom and Sue discovered when they had learned all the facts they needed to learn, they themselves had to do the work in order to make their dream come true.

So it must be for you. But our hope is that through this book, we can be helpful to you. It is for that purpose, and only for that purpose, that we have written it.

2
Setting the Stage

"Books," somebody once said, "are men's hearts in other men's hands." We like that thought. It certainly isn't true of books generally. But it *can* be true. We have read books that have deeply moved us, that have stirred us to new purpose, and that have even changed our lives.

The written word can be cold and lifeless. But it can come alive and glow. It can reach across the space that divides one person from another, and communicate warmth and understanding and caring. Letters can do the same. During World War II, we were totally separated for over three years. Those were dangerous years too, and we had no assurance that we would ever see each other, face to face, again. But we could write letters to each other, and we did. We poured out our hearts in some of those letters. Through the written word, we kept our relationship alive and communicated to each other our faith, our trust, our imperishable hope. We think our relationship actually grew during those long, grim years of total separation.

We can hardly hope to achieve that kind of communication through a book. We don't know you, our readers, as persons, and the communication is strictly one-way. In these circumstances, we could easily fail to say what you most need to hear; or worse, we could say something that, unknown to us, might hurt you. These are serious limitations, and we must accept the risks involved. But in spite of all that, we want to try to make this an experience of real interpersonal communication. We will do our best, and only you can judge how far we succeed.

Let us begin by introducing ourselves to you as a couple who, at the time of this writing, have been married for forty-four years. We won't bother you with a lot of detailed information, but will confine ourselves to basic facts. However, just in case you feel the need for further information, we have provided some at the end of the book. If you like, you can read this now or at some later time or not at all.

The basic fact is that we have spent most of our professional lives—at least forty years—trying to understand how marriages and families function. As professionals in the field, we have studied family relationships quite extensively—but not just for the sake of gaining knowledge or passing knowledge on to others. Our concern has always been to help marriages—and families—to be happier and better. We chose that, early on, as our goal in life, our vocation. We decided it would be the most useful way to spend our lives, and we have never doubted this.

We think we have the qualifications to be considered specialists in the field of marriage and the family. But we never feel quite comfortable in the "expert" role. We prefer to think of ourselves as a couple who have tried to make our own marriage work so that we could have something good to pass on to others. In the past we have functioned, together and separately, as teachers and counselors. But in later years we have preferred a simpler approach—sitting down informally with other couples, either as a foursome or in larger groups, and sharing our experiences of marriage in the hope that we could all help each other to learn and to grow. This has involved us deeply in what we now call the marriage enrichment movement, which we believe has exciting possibilities for a great increase in the sum of human happiness. We have written extensively about this elsewhere, and we have played an active part in founding the Association of Couples for Marriage Enrichment (ACME).

That should be enough by way of introducing ourselves. Now, what about you?

We see you as a married couple also. Ideally, you will be reading this book together and using it to work for the growth you want to achieve in your relationship. Other people, married or not, will read the book as individuals, looking, as it were, over our shoulders to see what is going on. But we shall talk—and talk directly and personally—to you as a married couple who are ready to join us in a quest—a quest for the growth of your marriage into a richly satisfying love relationship. We shall assume that this is what you are seeking, and our purpose will be to help you achieve it.

Beyond that, we shall not try to identify you precisely. We don't think of you as young, middle-aged, or old; as educated to any particular level; as belonging to any particular cultural or religious group. Over the years, we have worked with married couples in programs and projects in sixty-one different countries, and we have found that, deep down, beneath the cultural crust, they are all very much alike. All of us who enter marriage have very similar needs, very similar hopes, very similar frustrations. In the many couple-groups we have led, we have discovered that if we talk about our views and opinions concerning marriage, we get into endless differences and disagreements; but if we share our personal experiences of marriage, we all feel very close together and united. In our talks with you, therefore, we'll avoid as far as possible discussing views and opinions, and instead concentrate on what we have learned through experience.

We shall make no distinction, either, between couples who have "problems" and those who don't—for the simple reason that the distinction does not exist! We don't like the word *problem,* as it has come to be applied to marriage, and in this book we'll avoid using it as much as we possibly can. We will, however, use it now, but only to say that all couples *ought to* have problems, because if they don't, they don't have a real marriage at all, as we understand it. Marriage is a continuing struggle to turn the changing circumstances of life, and the inevitable conflicts that arise in every close relationship, into growth points for the improvement of the relationship. Consequently, we dislike talking about "good" and "bad" marriages; but if we must, we'd have to say that any marriage that is struggling to grow is good, and any marriage that has settled down to a state of nongrowth is bad.

So, whatever your marriage is like, according to your own expectations or according to the judgment of society, to us the important question is whether you are ready to work on it in order to make it better. If you are, we are ready to sit down with you and to see what we can learn from each other.

It may help us all if we emphasize the picture of sitting down together as the setting in which we will try to work. Six years ago, we built for ourselves a place of retreat in the mountains. It is there that we are writing this book. It is there that we have gathered many groups of couples for weekend retreats and training workshops. It is there that we have sometimes brought individual couples—to share our home as we all share each other's experiences. This is a form of marriage counseling that we like above all others—sitting in our living room, going down the mountain together for a meal at the old hotel, then back for another session until bedtime, and back to work again next morning. All status divisions are dropped; first names are used. We talk individually with one of you, with both of you; or all four of us talk together—whatever seems to be appropriate at any given time. There is no hurry, no pressure, no deadline to meet. And somehow, amid the undisturbed peace of the tall trees and the ageless mountains, we try to see our lives in perspective and to put everything all together.

What can we offer you?—only our help, our support, and our encouragement. *You* must do the work in your marriage, as we are doing in ours. But we also offer you confidence and hope. In working with couples in marriage enrichment, we have become very confident. We have become aware of the tremendous potential for change and growth that exists in all of us. We are impressed particularly with the resources for loving that we find in all people—often hidden away deep down, but always there. The limits to growth in your marriage are seldom in the marriage itself. They are in *you*. The limits can be expanded by your willingness to take what is available to you, to work for what you can achieve, to appropriate the potential that is already there waiting to be developed.

So great is our confidence that we would venture to say that if you will both sincerely and resolutely carry out the tasks we will define for you, and if you can be termed reasonably ''normal'' people, we can almost *guarantee* that you will ultimately achieve a happy marriage. And even if you don't quite fit that elusive normal category, hope need not be abandoned; because we can refer you to professional help that, at its best, can offer you resources today that have never been available before.

Please believe us when we assure you that we are not holding out to you any cheap or magical solutions nor claiming magical powers for ourselves. It is not in ourselves that this confidence resides. It is based on our belief that all people possess, in themselves, almost unlimited resources. What you can achieve in your marriage depends ultimately on what you *want* to achieve, and on what price you are ready to pay in terms of enlightened and sustained effort. In other words, we are now moving from an era in which marriages failed from lack of knowledge to an era in which the failure lies more and more in lack of the will to put knowledge to work. This means that the outlook for a really determined couple is now very, very hopeful.

3
What We Offer You

Most books give you *information*. We will do that. But what we offer is much more than that. We sincerely believe that we can promise you a more satisfying relationship (with solid results in the space of a few weeks) if you—both of you—will in turn promise to carry out faithfully the instructions we will give you.

This is not an empty promise. We are thinking of the couples we have been working with in marriage enrichment weekends now for fourteen years. In some, there has been quite dramatic improvement. But almost all have, over a six-month period, testified to a continuing progress. A research project, which tested the couples before and after their involvement in the weekend, left no doubt about the fact that their relationships had changed for the better. Other research projects on other couples involved in marriage enrichment programs have shown the same results.

However, the number of couples we can work with directly is very limited. We think we have something good to offer, and we would like to offer it to a much wider circle. A book seemed the best way to do this. Any couple can pick up a book, take it home, and use it as a guide. Books serve this purpose in many fields. We use books of instruction to become better gardeners, to improve our cooking skills, to learn to make household repairs, to become skilled in arts and crafts. So there seemed to be no reason why a book shouldn't likewise enable a couple to improve their marriage.

We know that there are already a few do-it-yourself books on achieving a successful marriage. We don't claim that this is the only one. Some of the things we shall say to you have been said before. Not many books, however, have used the direct, down-to-earth, practical, step-by-step approach we are using here.

All the same, we are well aware of some of the difficulties that confront us. We'd like to share them with you now—at the very start. Our guarantee doesn't hold unless the conditions are faithfully met on your side. Here are some of the things that could go wrong:

1. *You could read the book but not act on it.* This is all the more likely because it's the way we generally use books. We read them in what we call spare time, snatching them up when we get a chance, going through them as quickly as we can so that we can get on to the next task or the next book. As long as you think of a book as a source of information, that is acceptable. But, as we shall say again and again, in learning the great art of living, *information is almost useless unless it is translated into action.* All that happens as you read is that you conjure up fantasies of the happy, loving marriage you would like to have. You daydream that you have already achieved this, and this activity provides a pleasant escape from the dreary reality of having fallen far short of your hopes. Unless you act, the fantasy gradually fades, and you're back exactly where you started.

This is what happens to the vast majority of people who read books or hear talks or take part in discussions about marriage. It is, as the saying goes, "all in the mind." Nothing gets through to the "gut level," to the place where life is really lived, until you act. And acting to produce change and growth is always experimental, often risky, and sometimes painful. So it's very easy to stay with the fantasies and do nothing. You could read this book in that way. Perhaps many will. If so, we have to tell you quite frankly that it will make no significant difference in your life. Only if you act on what we tell you can it bring about the growth and change you wish for.

2. *One of you might be willing to do what the book tells you, but the other may not be willing to cooperate.* This is also a very real possibility. Getting individuals to take action is easier than getting couples to do so. To get a couple moving, two wills must go into action together. It's almost unbelievable how a married couple can get tightly locked into a pattern of living that is unsatisfying to both, is self-defeating, and is even downright destructive. Both may be vaguely aware of this, but they don't allow the awareness to surface; they dread the upheaval that could result if they really confronted the reality of their situation. So, in this unhappy state of affairs, they let the relationship drift helplessly, often to the point of no return. Thousands of marriages that could have been vital and fulfilling go this way, down and down to ultimate dissolution. Other couples are arrested in time by some major crisis that startles them into awareness of what they really knew all along but couldn't bring themselves to face.

We want to tell you now that we understand this state of paralysis that prevents a couple from taking action together. We have had to face it in our own marriage, and we will do our best to help you to break out of it. But we have to say to you, very firmly and very clearly, that it takes two people working together to get a marriage moving in the direction of growth and enrichment.

3. *You may both decide, halfheartedly, to make a start on improving your relationship, but you may not follow through.* Nothing can alter the fact that growth in a marriage means change, and change means work—sometimes quite hard work. We believe the rewards that can come to you will abundantly justify all your efforts, and we will give you all the encourage-

ment we can. But it will be necessary for you also—both of you—to believe this. Life can be very discouraging, and frequent failure can paralyze the nerve of effort. Then you can sink into hopeless, helpless lethargy and a mood of cynicism and despair. Many couples do this, and as a result, they throw away their chance of a satisfying life together.

We think it unlikely that you will be in this category, because in that event you would have had no motivation to read this book. But the danger is real that you may start working with us, begin to falter, get discouraged or distracted, and then give up. Having no direct contact with you, we have no means of reaching out a helping, sustaining hand if this should happen. We must simply recognize that this is a difficulty we both have to face.

Now let us try to be specific about our offer to help you.

It will be obvious to you that you'll have to give *time* to the task of building a better marriage. The story of Tom and Sue makes this very clear. But how much time could we reasonably settle for?

We have given considerable thought to this question. Our hope would be that you might set aside enough time to enable you to make some real progress. You'd have to do this at first as an investment, an act of faith. But very soon we'd hope to enable you to see some real gains. This could then encourage you to devote more time to the project, because you would know the project to be worthwhile.

What we propose is that you make a pledge to work with us for four hours a week during an initial, experimental period of six weeks. That means setting aside a total of twenty-four hours. And it means that even if you meet some discouragement at first, you won't give up until you have really tried for that length of time. Working with us for less time than that wouldn't really give us a fair chance; and if you take us seriously, we *expect* you to give us a fair chance.

We wouldn't want to schedule your time, during the six-week

period, in any rigid way. We'll make suggestions to you about using time fruitfully but leave you to interpret our instructions in ways that make sense to you. However, we'd expect you to make a genuine effort to free time to be alone together, and to give up some other claims in order to make this possible. In fact, our first call for action would be that you make a joint decision to take this project seriously enough to find time for it and to be really disciplined about it. If you're not willing to make this kind of commitment, we cannot, with the best intentions in the world, promise you anything.

All right, you say. If you agree to give us time, and to do what we ask of you, what do *we* promise you? Our reply is that we believe you will begin to move forward toward a happier, better, and more loving relationship. If that sounds rather vague, we'll try to spell it out in a little more detail here and give you a lot more detail later.

We offer you an opportunity to rekindle and deepen the love that brought you together in the first place. If you have had difficulty in communicating clearly with one another, if there have been areas of misunderstanding between you, if there are things you can't discuss together, we can promise you some real improvements. If you have been unable to resolve the inevitable conflicts that arise in any close relationship, if you have developed anger against each other and been unable to handle it constructively, if you have had difficulty in making effective decisions about your shared life, we can help you to make some real progress in these areas. If you have found it hard to express positive feelings to each other, to be affectionate and loving or to achieve interpersonal intimacy to undergird your sexual intimacy, we can offer you some ways of resolving these difficulties. If you have had trouble agreeing about your roles as husband and wife, in cooperating as partners in effective teamwork, or in defining how your personal lives and your shared life in marriage can be coordinated, we can offer you some hope of coming to grips with these adjustments. Remember, we can do none of

27

these things *for* you. But we can show you how to do them for yourselves, by offering practical steps that you should be able to take.

We can't estimate how much progress you can make, in these and other directions, in six weeks. But even in that short space of time, we believe you should be able to look back and see that you have begun to travel in the right direction—if you will do what we ask you to do.

Now we have to be very practical. Do you, or do you not, accept our offer by pledging your cooperation? If you feel uncertain, skim through the rest of the book and see what impression it makes on you. Please understand, however, that nothing gets started until you come back to where you are here and now and register your decision.

There is only one really effective way to do this. We ask you to make a contract with us. Here it is:

"We agree together to work with David and Vera Mace, through the book they have written, for the purpose of promoting growth and enrichment in our relationship as husband and wife, and to do so for a minimum period of six weeks from the time we sign this contract."

What we want you to do is to make your own copy of this agreement—either written or typed—and then both of you sign it and enter the date. Keep the document for future reference. It represents a contract you have made with one another and with us.

Please, this isn't a gimmick. We're not playing games with you. We are really serious. You could easily say that this is childish or that it's silly or that you don't like the idea. What we ask you to understand is that this contract represents action, and without your action we are powerless to do anything for you except give you information, which is going to be quite useless *unless you are willing to act on it.*

Your willingness to take this action is therefore the vital test of your sincerity. "A journey of a thousand miles," says the old Chinese proverb, "begins with one step." This is the step that can be, for you two, the beginning of a happier marriage. Are you willing to take it—together?

4
The Program Outlined

If you have taken the step we asked you to take at the end of the last chapter, it would be ideal if we could put you to work right away. But before that can happen, we have a number of things to explain to you; so our first instruction will have to be that you read on for several more chapters. What you are reading, however, will all have a direct bearing on the practical steps we shall then ask you to take.

After forty years of studying marriage, and after working in marriage counseling and marriage enrichment with thousands of couples, we have come to certain conclusions. Our main conviction is that there are three essentials for a happy marriage. These three together provide the means of success. Without them, success is much less likely; for most couples, impossible.

The three essentials are these:

1. A commitment to growth, sincerely entered into by husband and wife together
2. An effective communication system and the necessary skills to use it
3. The ability to accept marital conflict positively and to resolve it creatively

Each of these three is vitally important, and all three must go together. Possessing one without the other two, or even two without the third, is not enough. They supplement and support each other. The couple who want a happy marriage must achieve all three and sustain all three.

Given these essentials, all other areas of marriage can be managed successfully. The three essentials provide the basic equipment for resolving all other difficulties likely to arise in the relationship. Without the three essentials, there can be no effective resolution. For example, difficulties in such areas as sex, money, in-laws, gender roles, parenthood, decision-making, and the like, are only symptoms of a relationship that is not equipped to promote growth and change. If we try to make marriages function by dealing with these symptoms, we may achieve temporary relief, but trouble may only recur or break out somewhere else. The couple with the three essentials have the necessary equipment for dealing with almost any trouble likely to arise in their relationship. The couple without the three essentials may easily be caught short when some change in their life situation occurs, because they lack the equipment for overcoming obstacles.

There are a few exceptions to this general rule—but not many. Some individuals, as a result of unfortunate past experiences, find themselves unable to function in the complexity of *any* intimate relationship. Such people need personal therapy. Some couples need enlightenment and guidance about specific areas of marriage, such as sexual functioning and parenthood, before they can use their basic skills effectively in these areas. But in general, the three essentials are the key to successful marriage. Unfortunately, large numbers of married couples today lack these essentials. This explains why so many marriages are failing.

Our contract with you, during the next six weeks, will be to help you to build these three essentials into your marriage. In making the contract to work with us, you have already taken an important step toward the first essential, although we shall have to help you understand more clearly what marital growth is all about. Once we have done that, we'll show you how to learn effective couple communication and how to handle your

31

conflicts creatively. By means of these steps, we'll put you on the road that leads to the happy marriage you desire. Continued growth in the months and years ahead should then be possible.

Now we must talk in practical terms about what we'll be asking you to do. In the next three sections of the book, we'll try to give you, as simply and clearly as possible, the information you will need. But remember, the information does nothing for you until you act on it. You can think of it as a map of Europe, issued to you before you take a trip across the Atlantic. You can study the map carefully and learn much about Europe—the frontiers, the coastlines, the mountains and rivers, the railroads and highways, the cities. But all this will not begin to have personal meaning for you until you get on the plane and actually land in Europe.

So, when you have read what we have to tell you about how a healthy marriage functions, we'll ask you right away to begin putting it all into practice in your own relationship. We'll give you exercises to do—alone and together. These exercises, as you will see, are intended to get you into action. They are like the trips your European guide would arrange for you, so that the things you have studied on the map may become real to you by being actually experienced.

Some of the exercises may prove more helpful than others. But we want you to try them all. If you find ways of changing them a little to suit your own individual needs, go ahead. But each exercise has an important purpose and a special way of fitting into the total program. We'll try to make this clear as we go along.

A number of the exercises will ask both of you to write something down before talking to each other. This may seem artificial—why write when you are available to each other to talk? There is a very good answer to this question. All but the most mature couples have difficulty in talking freely and frankly to each other in sensitive areas. They may be afraid to say what they really think for fear of being put down or rejected. They may become self-conscious and unable to think clearly in each other's presence. They may find anger and resentment stirred up as they interact.

Putting your thoughts on paper is an excellent way of clearing your mind, of being really objective, and of confronting honestly what you think or feel. Just believe us when we say that this is really helpful; we're pretty sure you'll come to agree with us when you have given it a fair trial. A lot of trouble arises in marriages because husbands and wives speak out before they really examine their thoughts and feelings; harsh words are uttered that only arouse needless hostility. Writing first and speaking later, especially when sensitive issues are being dealt with, can often remove the obstacle to effective communication.

The program that follows gives you specialized assignments for each of the six weeks. These are arranged so that at each stage you build on what you have learned and experienced before. We suggest that you follow the order quite closely— although you can adapt the plan to your own particular needs if it doesn't seem to be working for you. Couples differ so much that no prepared plan can exactly suit them all. So change the order a little if you feel you must, but don't leave anything out. Every step is important.

To carry out this program, you *must* manage to set aside time alone together. We know how really difficult this can be, but all obstacles must somehow be overcome. The sessions you will schedule for sharing thoughts and feelings demand seclusion and freedom from interruption. A telephone call, a child's legitimate question, a neighbor stopping by—these normally accepted events could break into a sensitive and vital discussion and completely spoil it. So plan to find a place, as well as a time, that will be secure from any possible interruption. At an appropriate point, spending a night (or even a weekend) in a motel may lead to a significant breakthrough in your relationship. Other ways of finding seclusion are driving out to a remote spot, eating in an out-of-the-way restaurant, or taking a country walk together.

In all your sessions, make it a rule to *emphasize the positive.* We absolutely insist on this for the first two weeks. Many couples have unconsciously fallen into the habit of unloading negative feelings on each other, or even of putting each other down. No useful steps toward marriage enrichment can be taken in that kind of atmosphere. Even after you have done the communication exercises, when you do begin to look at some of your negative feelings about the relationship, play it cool. Let us offer you a useful device that we have often suggested to couples with whom we have been counseling. If at any time during a session together as a couple, one of you finds himself nearing the limits of his tolerance, he should silently raise one hand; and at that signal, without another word, you should both immediately break off the discussion and not resume it until the tension has died down. To go on beyond that point invariably turns out to be damaging and unprofitable. Raising the hand is somehow easier than trying to explain, and the signal should be acted on silently, with no further discussion of the subject.

Don't expect miracles. Progress may be slow at first. Long-established habits are not easily changed. You will make progress, then slip back, many times. Refuse to be discouraged by setbacks. Leave the past behind, and look with hope to the future.

Finally, get it clearly into your heads that you can change your behavior, almost without limit, when you are completely convinced that it is in your best interests to do so. We once asked Dr. James Peterson, who has directed one of the largest research projects on aging, what was the most significant thing he had learned about elderly people. He replied that his biggest surprise had been to discover that a person's power to adapt to new situations continues until the very end of life. When we say we *can't* change our ways of behaving, what we really mean is that we *won't.* Given enough motivation—and the conviction that something is really in our self-interest—we can all change and grow in new directions.

This is particularly true in marriage. Our basic personalities are fixed and unalterable. But our *behavior* (which is the way we use our personalities to relate to others and to gain the rewards we need for our happiness) can be adapted in a thousand ways. The reason so many husbands and wives fail to adapt themselves to each other is not that they can't, but that the idea of marital growth has had no recognition until now, and they have therefore not been encouraged to make the effort. Once we recognize that changes in relationships are not only possible but inevitable, we begin to realize that we have the power to direct those changes toward the achievement of mutual happiness. It is exactly this process that we are now inviting you to begin.

Now, read on. Each of the next three parts of the book will begin with reading material, followed by detailed instructions about what we ask you to do in your time alone together.

PART II
An Honest Look at Your Relationship

5
How Marriages Can Grow

Talk to an average couple about *marital growth,* and their minds go blank. We've tried it, and they've told us so! They have no frame of reference into which to fit such an idea. Likewise, the idea of measuring their marriage potential leaves most couples completely bewildered.

Why is this so?—because our culture has in the past taken a *static* view of marriage. It is described by the church and in the law as a "state" or "estate," a "condition" into which two people enter through a religious or legal ceremony. One day you are not married, the next day you are married—you have crossed a frontier, moved from one territory into another. The implication is that some dramatic change has taken place.

All this may be true *socially* but not *personally.* You are virtually the same person the day after your wedding as you were the day before. Changes will indeed come, but only over a period of time—months and years. And you have the power—and the responsibility—to guide and influence these changes. But you must also *do* something about them. If you don't act to "take hold" of the relationship, it will, like a rudderless ship, simply drift wherever the currents carry it.

What we are saying here is that *a wedding is not a marriage.* We'll repeat this for emphasis—*a wedding is not a marriage.* A wedding marks the beginning of a relationship that may or may not develop into a marriage. Not all do. The fact that about a million couples get divorced each year testifies eloquently to this fact. All of them have had a wedding, but they finally decided that they had been unable to achieve a marriage.

Let's use a simple illustration. Suppose the two of you had a great ambition to have a beautiful garden of your very own—a place of peace and serenity with tall trees, shapely shrubs, verdant lawns, and multicolored flowers—perhaps a rockery, a pool, a fountain. Now suppose we said to you, "We know about your dream, and we want to make it possible for you to have that garden. We have arranged to give you a piece of vacant land. Here is the title deed. It's yours, your very own."

Suppose you thanked us, then went to buy a couple of deck chairs, brought them back and set them down on your piece of land, and waited together for your garden! How long would you have to wait?

Of course, merely waiting wouldn't bring it. You'd have to do a lot of learning—about soil chemistry, about suitable plants, and about the art of arranging and planting. You'd have to develop new skills. You'd have to devote time and hard work to the task. And you would have to keep all this up for years. But if you did all this, one day your dream would really come true, and you would invite us to come and see your beautiful garden.

This is all so obvious that it would never occur to us to think otherwise. Yet we don't think that way about a marriage, do we? We somehow expect it all to happen (in some miraculous way) just because we say "I do." Is it any wonder that marriages are failing on every hand?

But marriages didn't fail in the past, did they? No—because nobody promised anyone a rose garden. Our culture took the view that *stability* was the mark of a satisfactory marriage. As long as the couple stayed together, they met the requirements of a marriage; and the power of religion, law, and public opinion saw to it that they did stay together. As to the quality of the relationship, nobody paid much attention to that. Marriage was clearly understood to be a duty. Whether it brought you happiness or not wasn't important. You did your duty and stayed with it.

Certainly, that was good for social order. But whether we like it or not, our expectations of marriage today insist that it shall be a loving, happy, rewarding relationship. If it doesn't turn out that way, most people give up.

But whose responsibility is it to make marriage a happy relationship?—the responsibility of the couple, surely. But since our culture hasn't yet faced the fact that duty will no longer hold people together, we're really trying to work a new system by obsolete methods. Instead, we should accept the fact that couples today not only expect a loving relationship but can be helped to achieve it. This is entirely possible—but we just haven't been doing anything about it. We must begin soon—or else!

If a wedding is not a marriage, and the making of a marriage is a long and complex task, then obviously the first essential for a successful marriage is a solemn commitment on the part of the couple to ongoing growth. We are entirely convinced that this is, and must be, the starting point. Until husband and wife have looked into each other's eyes and solemnly declared to each other that they will work together to the utmost of their powers to create a deep, rich, satisfying relationship of intimacy and love—until this decisive event takes place, you can't reasonably expect a marriage to develop out of a wedding.

But don't couples take wedding vows? Yes, they do—but the vows say little or nothing about growth. They are all about duty. They pledge to stay with each other whatever happens—for better or worse. We can find nothing in the wedding service about the power of the couple to see that it turns out better and not worse. So they walk out bravely, to the music of the wedding march, committed to take what comes, but *not* committed to work for growth and for the shaping of their own destiny. Is it any wonder that in the months and years that follow they just drift with the tide? The very language we use is significant—you get married and then "settle down."

Now the truth about marriage is that it is a very complex interaction between two very complex personalities that can be shaped and adapted and adjusted in thousands of different ways. The stability concept is completely out of touch with reality. Nothing that is alive and moves remains the same; it grows, it changes, it adapts, it develops its potential.

If we are to be realistic about marriage, then, we must rethink its whole meaning in relation to the growth concept. Consider how any marriage—and the marriage partners—are bound to change and grow.

1. Each person grows as his individual potential develops.
2. Each person changes in continuous adaptation to the other and to changes in the other.
3. Both persons change in response to changing cultural environments.
4. Both persons change in adaptation to the successive phases of the life cycle.

These are very complicated processes. They can't be entirely controlled, but it makes an enormous difference whether a married couple simply submit blindly to the processes of change and growth or whether they cooperate in directing these processes toward meeting their needs and achieving their goals.

But *can* they do this? Emphatically, yes. One of the most dramatic recent developments in the field of psychology has been in the area of what is called behavior modification. In recent studies of the outcome of marriage counseling, for example, use of this approach seems to show better results in clearing up marital difficulties than any other method.

The human potential movement points us in the same direction. We are now seeing how much power we have to shape ourselves in order to meet our deepest needs and to achieve our most important goals. We shall have more to say about this in the next chapter.

The old idea was that when people married, their behavior patterns became fixed, completely unchangeable. So you had to have people marry who were *compatible* with one another. If they weren't, they just had to put up with misery or give up and try again. We ourselves never quite accepted these rigid concepts. Years ago, we used to say—half in jest—"Compatibility in marriage is not so much a state of affairs as a job of work." Now we believe there is a great amount of truth in this. What you have, on your wedding day, is just a heap of raw materials. Your task is then to work on the relationship, and through the natural processes of change, adaptation, and growth, to shape the marriage of your dreams.

All this was beautifully expressed, years ago, in a poem by an Englishwoman known as Jan Struther. Here it is.

> The raw materials of love are yours—
> Fond hearts, and lusty blood, and minds in tune:
> And so, dear innocents, you think yourselves
> Lovers full-blown.
>
> Am I, because I own
> Chisel, mallet and stone,
> A sculptor? And must he
> Who hears a skylark and can hold a pen
> A poet be?
> If neither's so, why then
> You're not yet lovers. But in time to come
> (If senses grow not dulled nor spirit dumb)
> By constant exercise of skill and wit,
> By patient toil and judgement exquisite
> Of body, mind and heart,
> You may, my innocents, fashion
> This tenderness, this liking, and this passion
> Into a work of art.

We recommend that you read the poem slowly, twice over, and then ponder its meaning. What it says is profoundly important to all married couples.

6
Marital Growth in Our Changing Culture

These are exciting days in which to live. But one of the complications of being alive today is that you have to handle your own change and growth at the same time that the culture around you is undergoing profound change as well. It reminds us of the circus act in which the acrobat is trying to keep his balance on the back of the horse, while the horse is careering around the ring!

For many couples today the question of growth is closely tied up with the very controversial issue of women's liberation. Since the two are quite closely associated, we must take a look at what this is all about.

One important way that was used in the past to keep marriage stable was to make it a one-vote system. Experience showed that just as a nation was best held together when ruled by a powerful chief or king, so family relationships produced less conflict when one member made all the major decisions. That member, of course, was usually the husband-father. We call these families patriarchal, which means that the father was the boss!

Some patriarchs, like some kings, have been wise and benevolent rulers. Others have been cruel tyrants. In the rigid, closed societies of the past, however, the system of one-man rule, with all its deficiencies, worked reasonably well.

However, today we live in open societies that try to practice democracy, and one expression of democracy is seen in the liberation movements that have championed the status of workers, of colonies, of minority groups, of youth—and of women. And recently the movement for women's rights has zeroed in on the status of the wife. Some extreme things have been said about this issue, but when due allowance is made for excessive zeal, the fact remains that in the past married women, by our present-day standards, suffered a good deal of injustice.

In order to correct this situation, many married women are being challenged to demand more freedom and more recognition. In some cases they are directly attacking their husbands. In turn, their husbands (since they didn't create the system, but merely inherited it) naturally become either angry or hurt by the aggressive attitudes suddenly developed by their wives.

This is all closely linked with the growth-potential idea. These wives are demanding the right to develop their "personhood," which they interpret as freedom to get away from such tasks as housework and motherhood (both of which they now see as confining and demeaning) and to become involved in activities outside the home, such as higher education, paid jobs, and social action. When this happens, it tends to make the husband feel humiliated, and it creates a vacuum in the home. The result is often bitter conflict, which can result in the breakdown of the marriage. It is doubtful that *any* married couples in North America today have been totally unaffected by these events.

As often happens, a counterrevolutionary movement has now developed. Some religious groups, for example, urge us to go back to the comparative peace of the "good old days" when husbands ruled the home and wives submitted meekly to their authority. At the same time, another movement is working from the opposite end, trying to liberate husbands to abandon their traditional masculine power and authority and to live in equality, peace, and contentment with their liberated wives.

Where do you two, as a couple, fit into this broad picture? Let's look at a few possibilities.

45

1. *You hold to the traditional view* and maintain the system that makes the husband the head of the house, with the wife comfortably accepting his authority. Many older couples are in this situation. They have become so accustomed to the roles they learned in early life that they have no wish to change. If you are in this category, we would see no reason to ask you to do so. If you are both happy with this arrangement, you can still work on other aspects of your relationship, leaving that one, as far as possible, undisturbed.

2. *One of you (probably the husband), maintains the traditional view,* but the other wants to change. Your situation is really a difficult one, and you had better take it seriously and work on it. In our experience, a husband or wife who independently feels the urge to give up the old system, in order to work for a companionship of equals, needs to understand that the other partner can only accept this change with considerable resentment, which is likely to stir up conflict and bitterness in the marriage, and eventually alienation. The best hope is for the partner who takes the traditional view to look with an open mind at the new pattern, while the partner who wants change tries to be helpfully persuasive rather than aggressive. A very useful experience for a couple in this situation is to get into a growth group with other couples who are making the companionship model work and see how it looks from the inside.

3. *You are both in the process of changing your marriage pattern* from the traditional to the companionship model. This certainly involves much growth and change, but since you are both traveling in the same direction together, it should be possible to make the transition fairly smoothly. It is important to realize, however, that moving from a one-vote to a two-vote system *inevitably introduces a great deal of new conflict into the relationship,* so the two of you will have to work hard at learning the creative use of conflict, which we shall be dealing with extensively later in the book.

4. *You are both committed to the companionship marriage*

and have very few hang-ups from the older model. This will be true of most young people today. If this is your situation, you should understand clearly, as we have already pointed out, that the new model has some real built-in hazards—particularly the excessive amount of interpersonal conflict that is inevitably involved—and also the risk that the disproportionate pursuit of individual freedom may rupture the relationship.

We would like to say something more about the last point. The great emphasis on personal freedom nowadays holds the danger that our society could swing from one extreme to the other. Let us explain what we mean.

The weakness of the older cultures was that, in order to gain strength and stability, they tended to produce tyrants, who ruled with an iron hand and denied individual rights. Ordinary men and women in those older societies were compelled to put their social duties before their individual rights. The penalties were so heavy that they had no alternatives if they wanted to survive.

The advent of democracy gradually overthrew the tyrants and produced societies in which individual rights and social duties were roughly balanced. This is what democracy means: as a group we champion the individual, and as a group we create a system that sees to it that the individual gives due consideration to the needs of others.

But now we are in danger of swinging to the other extreme—to the tyranny of a system in which individual rights come before social duties. Our passion for personal freedom today takes less and less account of our obligations to other people. The plea "I've got to be me" is used to justify an ugly disregard for the needs and rights of others. This is a powerful factor in the widespread cynicism about marriage that has developed in recent years. Increasingly, husbands and wives feel justified in walking out of marriage for relatively trivial reasons, giving little heed to the plight in which they place their partners and their children. This kind of "arrogant individualism" can dull our sensitivity to the commitments we have to the well-being of others who are integral parts of our lives. It is a good thing to work for one's own personal growth, but not at the cost of causing needless suffering to others. That is *not* personal growth in the true sense. It is the growth of egotism, accompanied by the decline of compassion and altruism. A society of people who have lost the willingness to make personal sacrifices for the well-being of others is no longer a democracy. The pendulum has swung to the opposite extreme, and we have exchanged one all-powerful tyrant for many petty tyrants.

We believe that marriage and family relationships provide us with the ideal setting for the best kind of personal growth. In a relationship in which we are fully known and also deeply loved, we can grow in a balanced fashion. A loving partner will not restrict our personal growth, but will do everything possible to promote it. But family obligations will restrain any growth toward egotism and will keep us constantly aware of our duty to forgo personal fulfillment when we could only secure it by denying the needs of others.

A happy, loving marriage, therefore, brings great rewards. It creates the ideal climate for simultaneous growth of the individual and of the relationship, each aspect supporting and enhancing the other. The view often expressed today, that marriage is confining and a hindrance to growth, must be challenged. This was certainly true of many of the rigid marriages of the past. It could be true of a shallow, insecure marriage today, in which jealous partners suspect each other, snoop on each other, clutch at each other. But it is no part of our purpose in this book to justify or support poor marriages. On the contrary, we are urging you to develop the kind of marriage in which things of this kind need not happen.

What about "open marriage"? We find the term a rather confusing one. To us it can have three different meanings. We certainly believe in the marriage in which the partners are open to each other, and we shall stress this again and again. We want also to promote marriages that are open to growth and creative change. We believe, too, that marriages should not be shut up within themselves, but should be open to the wider fellowship of mankind. We ourselves have discovered that our own lives have been greatly enriched by sharing with others what we have learned together. It is because of that conviction that we are writing this book.

The fact must be faced, however, that being open to growth and change inevitably involves some risks and may also involve pain. The great social changes taking place in our contemporary world are hard to live with. Yet when we balance some of the risks involved in living today against the rigid, sterile, and restricted lives that many people lived in earlier times, we can only feel glad to be alive in the contemporary world. We think the new understanding of growth and human potential that is coming to us holds out great promise for better and happier marriages in the future. Why wait, therefore, to appropriate these new and exciting ways of finding love and happiness? All that is needed is a commitment to growth and the determination to go on growing together—in a familiar phrase, "the will to make it work."

7
What's Your Marriage Potential?

Marriages—and people—can grow in two basic ways. One is the process of adaptation to the changing circumstances of our lives. We can be helped and encouraged when something we attempt turns out well, and we can be strengthened and refined by adversity. This kind of growth is a response to the world outside ourselves.

The other, more basic, kind of growth is a response to what is *inside* ourselves—our hidden, or latent, capacity to develop by drawing on our resources of personality and character.

We all know something about potential. Beethoven did not become a great musician just by taking lessons and practicing the piano. He "had it in him," as we sometimes say. We give children I.Q. tests in order to find out their built-in mental capacity—it wouldn't be kind to send kids with very low I.Q.'s to college. There seems to be some evidence, too, that certain people are suited by disposition for certain careers—that is part of what "vocational guidance" is about.

The human potential movement, as it is called, has developed in recent years in order to study people's capacity for growth and achievement. The idea is that if you have an innate capacity to

50

do something worthwhile, you ought to have the chance to reach the goal of which you are capable. A boy who has the potential to run the mile in under four minutes should get training for track events, and a girl with a flair for writing poetry should be encouraged to discipline and display her talent. Yet most of us, it seems, live far below our potential. Einstein once said that in the course of a lifetime, most people never use more than 10 percent of their intellectual capacity.

The idea of applying all this theory to relationships, and particularly to marriage, is quite new. Others may have thought of it before we did, but we only began to consider it seriously as a result of reading a rough estimate by Don Jackson, a psychiatrist we knew who had made some very extensive studies of American marriages. He ventured the opinion that the proportion of marriages that were really well developed was in the region of 5 to 10 percent. This made us wonder whether the more than 90 percent that weren't so well developed might have reached the same level. We don't know the answer, but the idea of marriage potential took root in our minds at that point, and we became more and more convinced that it opens up exciting prospects.

As we thought this over, there came into our minds a picture of the Indian peasant farmer. We know India well, having worked there on seven separate occasions. We had often seen the thin, emaciated figure of the peasant, a living skeleton in a loincloth, guiding his lumbering ox over his piece of land, pulling a crude wooden plow—just as his ancestors had done for centuries. Always near starvation, the peasant might have done much better for himself and his family if only he had known something about the scientific approach to agriculture—soil erosion, fertilizers, crop rotation, and so on. But he was doomed by his ignorance to a life of abject poverty; the miserable yield he got from his land could not provide his family with enough food for healthy living.

A startling thought occurred to us. Is it possible that in North

51

America, the wealthiest region of the world and in many ways the most advanced, millions of married people are like that Indian peasant? Because they don't understand how to develop healthy marital relationships, are they putting up with a miserable yield? In all of these people, there is the same human need for love, for warmth, for tenderness; for intimacy and companionship; for understanding and encouragement and support. Yet they are starved for these vital emotional nutrients, because their attempts to achieve fruitful and creative relationships are thwarted by ignorance. Nobody tells them how to develop and appropriate their marital potential.

We are now convinced that there is very much truth in this idea. Again and again in our marriage enrichment programs, we have seen couples with dull, dreary marriages who suddenly recognized the hidden possibilities in their relationships, learned how to develop their latent powers, and found that their marriages could "come alive" and start to grow. This has happened too often now (over more than a dozen years) for us to be in any doubt about it. There is an immense amount of marital potential around that never gets appropriated. We're inclined to think that Einstein's guess about people using only 10 percent of their intellectual potential might apply equally well to marital potential.

But what do we mean by marital potential? It all sounds so vague. How can you possibly study it—or measure it? That question has been a challenge to us, a challenge we have tried to meet.

No doubt, a number of psychological tests could be used, and in time this issue may all be explored scientifically. But meanwhile, we have been concerned not so much to sell this idea to the behavioral scientists as to put it across to married couples.

We have come up with a solution. We have developed a way to measure marital potential. It isn't an objective scientific measuring process (that will have to wait), but it enables couples to form a pretty good idea of where they are in their marriages, compared with where they could reasonably hope to be.

We'll describe the test right now, and we want you both to take it, later on, as part of your first work unit. You don't have to turn it in to an expert to be scored. You do that yourselves. It is very important that you each take the test separately—without collaborating or knowing what the other is doing. Then, and only then, may you plan a session of an hour or two in which you will put your results together, see how they compare, and draw the conclusions from them.

The test is surprisingly simple. All you do is list, on a sheet of paper, the following ten areas of the marriage relationship.

1. Common goals and values
2. Commitment to growth
3. Communication skills
4. Creative use of conflict
5. Appreciation and affection
6. Agreement on gender roles
7. Cooperation and teamwork
8. Sexual fulfillment
9. Money management
10a. Parent Effectiveness
10b. Decision-making

Notice that in the tenth area, two possibilities are given. This is to provide an alternative for couples who do not have children or are not currently involved with children.

Now you should try to estimate just where *your* marriage is in these ten areas, taking each one in turn and deciding upon a score from zero to ten for each area. To decide your score, you should consider what your relationship would be like if you had both together made all the progress you could possibly make in the area concerned, that is, learned all you could, worked together at it to the best of your abilities, sought all the outside help you might need. When you have formed an idea of what your marriage *could* be like, this would represent the full ten points. Next, consider where your marriage is *now*—how far you have already traveled toward the fulfillment of your full potential—and give yourself a score, from zero to ten, to represent your present level of achievement. Remember, you are scoring the *marriage*—not just your own part in it.

This should be done carefully and honestly. But be fair to yourselves and give yourselves credit for whatever you have already accomplished. One good way of doing this is to run fairly quickly through the list and spontaneously write in scores in pencil; then go back over them all more carefully and critically and change any scores you don't feel are exactly accurate.

When you have completed all your scores, add them up. This will give you the percentage of your estimated potential that you have already achieved. Subtract this from one hundred, and you will have the percentage of your marital potential that you still have to appropriate.

After you have both had adequate time to do this separately, schedule an uninterrupted period—we suggest one to two hours—to go over your scores together. First, compare your percentages of achieved potential. If they are very close, this means that you are both in fairly complete agreement about where your marriage is. If, on the other hand, there is a significant difference in your percentages, this means that your standards of evaluation are not the same, and it would be a good idea to find out why. Low scores can mean poor performances. But they can also mean high expectations. Differing views either of your performance or of your expectations need to be investigated—to see what lies behind them.

Now, go over your individual scores for each of the ten areas. Again, you may find some in close agreement. Wide differences need to be looked at together, and you may gain some important insights by discussing them. If in some areas you both have low scores, you can quickly agree that these are areas on which you have some work to do. Don't take a pessimistic view of low scores; they mean you have good things coming to you that you haven't yet claimed.

Most couples find doing this test a very revealing and very helpful experience. Most tell us that this is the first time they have ever really taken an honest look at where they are in their relationship. Some couples who thought they had an excellent relationship are quite surprised. One couple said: "We have been shaken out of our complacency. Now we've got to get to work."

We have found this test a convincing answer to some couples who defensively say, when the subject of marriage enrichment comes up: "Oh, we don't need anything like that! Our marriage is all right." Our reply would be: "That's fine. But wouldn't it be a good idea to find out just how all right it is?"

The test can be taken again over a period of time. We ourselves have done this, and we have noticed how we get fluctuations in our scores. Over time, a couple change their perceptions—both of their expectations and their levels of attainment. The test can help you to keep a check on the progress you are making in your marital growth.

We have explained this test in detail now, so as to give you some idea in advance of the kind of exercises that will be part of the program we are inviting you to share with us. We hope you will find the test revealing—and helpful. It should always be viewed *positively*—in terms of the good things that await you as you work together at raising your scores in areas in which you have fallen short.

Out of the marriage potential test has come the idea of a "growth plan." Once you are able to be specific about where your marriage is now, and about the directions in which you need to make further progress, it is possible for the two of you to draw up a definite plan for your future growth. We'll explain this more fully when the time comes.

We have talked with you about marital growth in theory, as well as in very practical terms. We are now ready to put some of this into action, in the first work unit of the program, which will cover the first two weeks of your contract.

8

Getting to Work— Together

You have made a commitment to work with us for six weeks. For each of these weeks, we shall give you a work unit outlining specific tasks to perform both separately and together. Two of these units will focus on each of the three essentials for a happy marriage. There will, however, be some overlap. For example, we will need to start you right away with some help on communication, although that will be dealt with much more fully later. Also, near the end of the program, we'll encourage you to go back and revise your earlier growth plan in the light of new insights you will have gained by then.

We can't hope that the "flow," or sequence, we suggest will be exactly right for all couples, because needs differ so much between one marriage and another. But we suggest that you keep pretty close to the schedule. All the things we are asking you to do are important, and it doesn't really matter if they don't come exactly in the order that is ideal for you.

Your Initial Reactions

We need to begin by asking you how you feel as you are about to embark on this program. There are three possibilities.

1. *Both of you are hesitant and reluctant.* This may be no more than the usual "butterflies in the stomach" you feel before taking a dive into cool water or getting up to make a speech. It can even be a sign that you are really taking this seriously, and that you are aware that a lot is going to depend on how it works out.

However, the reluctance may go deeper than that. You may be afraid that some things are going to come out into the open that you won't know how to handle. You may not be sure deep down that you really are willing to pay the price, in effort and commitment, for a more meaningful relationship. You may have no confidence that the two of you—even with the help this book can give you—will be able to make any real progress—you've tried before and been discouraged. You may even, deep down, have real doubts about whether this marriage can ever amount to much.

If feelings of this kind are bothering you, they had better be faced. We wouldn't want you to go ahead with serious mental reservations—it probably wouldn't work anyway. So if you made the commitment in all sincerity, but you now want to reconsider it or postpone it, by all means do so.

If you both decide not to go ahead, however, this will have some consequences. You wouldn't have signed that contract if part of you didn't really want to improve your marriage. And that part of you is going to feel let down, so that you will have some sense of failure to live with. This also needs to be faced.

If, therefore, you both feel hesitant about going ahead, we strongly urge you to find out what's going on. The best way would be for each of you, separately, to sit down quietly and write out a statement of what you are feeling about this, and why. Then, get together and report to each other, as fully as you can, what you have found out. Then try to reach an agreement about what to do next.

It may be that you just don't have any confidence in your ability to work on your marriage together. If that is so, you may be missing all the good things that could come out of growth in

58

your relationship, and it might be a good idea to find a counselor who could help you to get started.

2. *One of you is willing to go, the other is not.* It may comfort you to know that this is not at all an unusual state of affairs. In our marriage enrichment weekends, we even have a name for the unwilling partner—the "dragee"! We go out of our way to honor the dragee for an act of special love and loyalty—he did something against his own inclination in order to please his partner. That's worthy of recognition. We would likewise want to salute, right now, the one of you who feels reluctant but is willing to go on for the sake of the other.

It might or might not be helpful to talk this over first. You must decide. But we would strongly urge you to go ahead with the work schedule. The dragee should try his or her best to get involved in the program, and the other partner should respond with all possible gratitude, appreciation, and encouragement. It is our almost invariable experience that dragees, as they become involved, begin to get really interested, and they usually end up as enthusiastic about what they are doing as their partners.

3. *Both of you are ready and eager to begin.* This is obviously the desirable state of affairs, and we need not make any further comments.

Objectives of Units for First and Second Weeks

Our overall goal is quite clear. It is to get you started together in ongoing marital growth. In the chapters you have just read, what this means is clearly explained. If you have any uncertainty about this, read them again.

In order to get off to a good start, we want to stress a few particular objectives for these units.

1. *We want you to begin by taking a good look at your marriage as it now is.* Surprisingly enough, many couples have to admit that they have never done this before. We ask you to do it

now because it's the only sensible way to start. We'll offer you several different ways of looking at your marriage. By the end of your first two weeks in the program, you should know pretty clearly where you are.

2. *We want you, in everything you do in these next two weeks, to keep the emphasis entirely positive.* We are asking you to do this for a very good reason. In this beginning period, we want you to find the experiences enjoyable and encouraging. Many married couples get into the habit of being very negative in their communications with each other. If this is in any sense true of you, we want to beg of you, just for two weeks, to shut off the negative and emphasize the positive.

If you say this would be artificial, we agree. But we still want you to do it. We're not running away from the negative issues. We'll come to them later, but only when we can give you some tools to deal with them constructively. Meanwhile, for just two weeks, we want you to turn on your very best behavior! Don't say you can't do this—you can. Every businessman can be charming to a prospective customer. Every wife, whatever she feels inside, can be friendly to a neighbor who stops by. Anyway, you probably both managed to behave graciously toward each other, for at least part of the time, before you were married! See if you can do it again.

So, for two weeks, try to create an atmosphere of harmony and peace. Show only the best side of yourselves to each other. This isn't just a gimmick. You both have plenty of pleasant and charming qualities, and it's going to be helpful to emphasize them right now.

You may slip up. A nasty remark may slip out through your defenses; an unkind act may happen before you can stop it. In that event, take it back at once. Apologize. Then, without delay, do or say something positive to cancel it out.

Norman Vincent Peale once wrote a book called *The Power of Positive Thinking*. It's still widely read. One of the ways to encourage positive thinking is to practice positive acting. We want you to do that, to the best of your ability, for the next two weeks.

3. *We want you, in all your discussions, to look forward hopefully.* A favorite game with many married couples is to list each other's past errors. Sentences beginning with "You always..." and "You never..." are usually followed by a catalog of the partner's vices. We have all made mistakes, fouled things up, said unkind things, acted mean, failed to carry out our promises, let people down, made fools of ourselves, at one time or another. Anyone who lives close to us and knows about these past misdeeds possesses a powerful and very hurtful weapon that can be used against us.

We ask you, as you embark on this program, deliberately and purposefully to put this weapon aside. The past is past. What matters is the future, which now stands as a clean slate before you. We just don't have to repeat in the future all our errors of the past. We have the power to change, to act differently, to do better. What we are asking you to do with us, as a couple, is to restructure your lives so that in the future you gradually give up ways of behaving that have only made you both miserable, and to replace them with new and better patterns. So don't drag in your partner's past misdeeds—or even your own! You have the power, working together, to change your marriage. Start planning now for a better and happier future together.

By way of materials, all you will need for the work units is—for each of you—an exercise book (or large notebook) in which to write down some of your reflections, and a reliable means of checking on the time—a clock or watch with a minute hand or, better still, a portable oven timer.

9

Work Units for First and Second Weeks

We are now ready to give you detailed directions for the first two weeks of our program together. We'll begin with the schedule for the first week, followed by directions. Then we'll do exactly the same for the second week.

Each week of the program should begin with a session of at least two hours in which you can be alone together in a pleasant setting free from interruption. Plan this carefully in advance. For most couples, it will probably be easiest to clear this stretch of time during a weekend—let's say Saturday. We'd like you to set the stage by doing something pleasant together beforehand— like dining out at a favorite restaurant and talking about things you enjoy together. For this purpose, you may relax the rule about going back to the past, as long as you confine the discussion to *happy* experiences!

What we're asking you to plan is a weekly "date"—an especially purposeful one. Why shouldn't married couples have weekly dates? If your children want to know what's going on, tell them plainly that you're going out together on a date. They have their times out with their friends, and you are likewise entitled to have yours.

Following the two-hour Saturday session, we want you to

decide how you will set aside twenty minutes each day during the next week (Sunday to Friday). We'll explain how this time is to be used later.

In order to avoid any possibility of your participation becoming one-sided, we suggest that you alternate in leading the sessions and in keeping the time. We will include a reminder in the schedules (*H* for husband, *W* for wife) for your guidance.

Two hours on one chosen day and twenty minutes on each of the following six days—that's a total of four hours each week. For the whole six-week period, this adds up to a total of just twenty-four hours. This is the amount of time we want you to invest in getting started on the road that should lead to a happy marriage. That's your contract, and we expect you to fulfill it.

Schedule for First Week

Preparation: Read or reread chapters 5, 6, 7, and 8.

Saturday: Two-hour session
First hour (H leads)—Evaluation exercise
Second hour (W leads)—Bargaining session

Sunday to
Friday: Twenty minutes daily—Ten and Ten (H and W lead alternate days.)

Directions

We will now describe what we call the evaluation exercise. It is intended to get you started in taking an honest look at your marriage as it now is. You should spend about an hour in doing and discussing the exercise.

When you are settled comfortably in a relaxed atmosphere and are ready to begin, you should each take your notebook and write down the following:

1. Three to five things about your marriage that you think are very good, that make you feel happy and satisfied
2. Three to five things in your marriage that could be even better than they are—areas in which there is room for improvement
3. Three to five specific things that you personally could do to make the marriage better and happier than it now is

Give yourselves about fifteen minutes to work on this. Do it in a reflective, unhurried way. When you have finished, share with each other what you have written—first both sharing your reflections about the first section, then moving to the second section, finally moving to the third.

Discuss together how you react to each other's reflections. How far do you seem to be in agreement? If you differ in your evaluations, try to find out why. Has the exercise brought to light anything new about the way you both see the marriage? Do you want to modify your evaluations in any way after hearing the other person's point of view?

When you take the marriage potential test later on, you'll have a chance to look at your relationship in much greater detail. This simpler exercise is intended to start you off in the evaluation process.

For your second hour together, we have scheduled a bargaining session. The focus will now be on the third section of the evaluation exercise that you have just done. We'd like you to use this material to get yourselves into action right away.

Bargaining plays an important part in marriage, and we'll have more to say about this later. Right now, we want you to make a small experiment together. Both of you have listed some things you personally could do to improve your marriage. If you as an individual actually undertake to carry out a change, this should please your partner and you deserve to be rewarded. A suitable reward would be for your partner, in return for what you undertake, to undertake something that would please you.

We suggest that you try to work out such a deal together and put it into action for just one week. Together you can work out something that really will be a fair exchange, and welcome on both sides. Whatever is agreed upon, it should be reasonable as well as possible to carry out; it should represent a positive improvement in the relationship; and each partner should consider it a fair bargain. The deal would be for a limited period only and thus be open to renegotiation.

What we are getting into here is a very simple experiment in behavior modification. We want to give you encouragement by showing you that, when sufficient incentive is provided, you both *can* change your behavior. Even if the change is a very small one, it will give you hope that over time, and with full cooperation, much greater changes can eventually take place.

So see if you can work out one agreed change on each side, just for this week. If nothing you wrote in the exercises will do, explore other possibilities. Try to reach an agreement on *something* you can both change right away.

For the rest of the week, we want you to commit yourselves to doing the Ten and Ten. Some of you may already know what this is. It was developed by the Catholic Marriage Encounter as an outcome of the couples' weekends it organizes. After the weekend is over, couples are asked to engage in a daily dialogue, so that they can begin to be in real touch with each other's thoughts and feelings. The Ten and Ten has been found to be an excellent way of structuring this, and we would like you to use it.

Here's what you do. For ten minutes each day, each of you writes down, in your notebook, your "reflections"—thoughts and feelings about yourself, about each other, and about your relationship. You can do it separately, at times to suit yourselves. Then you get together, at an agreed time, for ten minutes; you exchange notebooks, each read what the other has written, and talk about your reactions. Be sure to keep your notebooks; you're going to need them quite often later.

What we are trying to do here is to open the channels of communication between you. Because of our special emphasis at this point, remember to keep clear of negative material and destructive criticisms of each other. With that exception, try to bring out your real thoughts and feelings and to be honest about them.

Arrange the times that suit you best. But accept the discipline of *doing this every day* for the next week. Don't let any unexpected event, or any discouraging incident, cut you off from your daily dialogue.

Just to help you get started, here is a specimen of what one husband and wife shared one day. It may not be your style, but perhaps it will give you the general idea.

Specimen of Ten and Ten Dialogue

HUSBAND: I've been feeling tired today, and this has affected my mood. I wasn't very sociable at work, and once I snapped at my secretary. So when I came home, I felt grouchy. I see now that it would have been much better to tell you and the kids that I wasn't in a good mood. When Johnny tried to tell me about the art exhibit they are planning at school, I am afraid I didn't show any enthusiasm, and I guess he felt let down. I know you were aware of this, because I saw you looking sadly at us. You might have bawled me out for this, but you didn't, and I want to thank you for your restraint. In the mood I was in, I wouldn't have taken criticism well.

All of this comes of hiding my real feelings. It would have been much better to say what was on my mind—I might have even gained a little sympathy! But there's a streak in me that won't let me admit when I am hurting. I guess it's my masculine ego.

They tell us to keep a stiff upper lip, but they don't tell us not to be bad-tempered at home while we're doing so!

I'd like you to help me to be more free to tell you when I'm feeling grouchy—just so you know what the score is. It isn't that I want sympathy—well, that isn't really true—I *do* want sympathy. But I *don't* want to be pitied!

Let's talk about this sometime.

WIFE: At a store in town today, I was very tempted to buy a dress that was going at a bargain price. I even tried it on. But I was pretty sure you wouldn't approve, because we've been talking about our finances lately and deciding we need to be more economical. I had some very mixed feelings about this. Before we started working on our marriage, I think I would have just bought the dress and "toughed it out" with you. But somehow I couldn't do that—I'd have felt I was being mean and letting you down.

I began to look into my feelings and to ask myself why I wanted the dress anyway. I could have argued that I needed it. But I knew it would be disloyal to you (at a time when we are trying to cut expenses) to buy it. So I didn't. I came home with mixed feelings— some frustration, but also a sense of virtue. Before, I don't think I'd have told you anything about this— pride or cussedness or what? But now, I feel I would like you to know about it. And I'd like you to express appreciation of the little victory I gained. Is it reasonable to ask for that?

The fact that I can write this down for you to read gives me a good feeling. I think we are learning to be much more open in sharing our inner thoughts with each other. I'm glad about that—aren't you?

Schedule for Second Week

Preparation: Reread all Ten and Ten reflections for the first week.

Saturday: Two-hour session
First hour (W leads)—Take marriage potential test separately, then report to each other.
Second hour (H leads)—Further discussion of marriage potential test. Start on growth plan.

Sunday to
Friday: Continue daily Ten and Ten (H and W lead alternate days).

Directions

We now want you to follow up the evaluation exercise you did last week with the marriage potential test, which will give you a much more detailed look at your marriage. You will remember that this was described fully in chapter 7, and you'll find there all the information you need to take it.

After taking the test and reporting your scores to each other, you should use what you have learned to make a rough growth plan. Just list some of the areas in your relationship in which you find room for improvement, and consider some ways in which you could get to work in achieving more of your potential. Put your findings in writing and keep them until later, when we will be asking you to make a much more detailed growth plan. By that time, you will have learned some new skills that will be useful in achieving your goals. But it will be helpful now to take a preliminary look at what these goals might be.

During this coming week, we'd like you to continue the Ten and Ten daily.

PART III
Learning to Communicate Effectively

10
Can You Hear Me, Darling?

The Family Service Association of America once made a careful four-year study of American families (see Dorothy Fahs Beck and Mary Ann Jones, *Progress on Family Problems* [New York: Family Service Association of America, 1973]). It included a section on why marriages go wrong. This national organization has over three hundred affiliated counseling agencies across North America staffed by hundreds of skilled and experienced marriage counselors. These counselors were asked to complete questionnaires in which, among other things, they listed the main causes of marriage troubles among the couples with whom they had worked.

The findings of the counselors were then combined to show the frequency with which the different problem areas occurred. Of course, any one couple counseled could (and obviously did) have difficulties in several of these areas.

In the list of causes, we can find all the usual things we blame for marriage failure—conflicts over children, sex, money, leisure, relatives, and infidelity. One or more of these occurred in an average of about 35 percent of all of the couples. Other difficulties, like housekeeping conflicts and physical abuse, were lower on the scale, an average of 16 percent. However, far above all the rest, way up at the 86-percent level, in splendid isolation, we find an item that many people would not expect. Yes, you guessed it. The item is difficulties with communication. Again and again the counselors reported that husbands and wives complained, "We can't talk to each other."

Most people, we believe, would be surprised by this. Ask the average married couple if they are able to communicate, and they will probably reply, "Of course we can." They may even feel that the question is just a little impertinent.

Of course, it all depends on what we mean by communication. Most people would interpret communication as the exchange of information: "You sound cheerful"; "Looks like it's going to be a hot day"; "Did you know the Browns have bought a new car?"; "I'll be home a bit later than usual tonight."

This kind of communication is easy enough, although even at that level things can go wrong! But of course the failures in communication about which these counselors were talking were at the deeper levels: communicating feelings, expectations, intentions, and personal needs. It's in these areas that married couples, again and again, fail to get through to each other. Often they don't even try; they don't consider this part of being married. And the result, as the major study shows, is that plenty of marriages are in trouble.

Many of us fail to realize that couples living together need a much more sensitive system of communication than we ever learn in the wider life of society. In our ordinary daily contacts with other people, we are continually practicing deception or withholding the truth. When you meet a friend in the street and he asks you how you are, you automatically say, "Fine, thank you." If you were to tell him the truth—that you have a headache, a stiff left arm, and an ingrowing toenail, he'd hardly know how to respond! You don't tell people about personal things like that; it just isn't done. When your neighbor shows you her new wallpaper, you say something appreciative, even if you really think it is hideous. Holding back your real feelings—and even the true facts—is simply part of our accepted social code of behavior. And it can be justified—our relationships with these people are not intimate and personal. Only a small part of their lives touches an equally small part of our lives. So there is no need to disclose our more private selves to them.

However, marriage is an entirely different kind of relationship. It brings two people together—in the closest possible intimacy— to share each other's lives and to try to meet each other's interpersonal needs. In that kind of relationship, an altogether different system of communication is required. Unfortunately, our training in wider social relationships gives most of us very little chance to learn the more intimate kind of communication. Psychiatrist Rudolf Dreikurs once said that there is nothing in our culture that prepares us for an intimate relationship like that of marriage.

How, then, are we to learn? The sad truth is that most of us never do. Even in marriage, husbands and wives build the same walls of insulation around themselves that people do outside the home. They long for intimacy, love, and tenderness. But the price is being open and being vulnerable—and protecting our inner lives has become so habitual to us that we can't bring ourselves to pay that price, even for what we eagerly want and desperately need.

But that isn't the whole story. A good amount of feeling is in fact expressed in families—probably a lot more today than ever by our tight-lipped ancestors. But the sad fact is that much of it is *negative* feeling. When married couples, and parents and children, disapprove of what is said and done in the home, and feel hostile, they usually don't hesitate to criticize and blame each other. Yet when they feel warm, tender feelings for each other, they are usually too embarrassed to say anything at all. So negative feelings get full expression, and positive feelings get very little expression. There is some truth in the story of the

73

elderly husband who, on his golden wedding anniversary, was asked by a news reporter, "And do you still love your wife after all those years together?" His reply was, "Yes, sir, indeed I do. In fact, there are times when I have a real hard job not telling her so!"

Ian Suttie, a British psychologist, wrote a book called *The Origins of Love and Hate.* He had a lot to say about the "taboo on tenderness" that exists in our Western culture, and especially in the Anglo-Saxon part of it. Men particularly have great difficulty in expressing appreciation and affection that they feel for their wives.

So it seems that in our families, emotional communication tends to be much more negative than positive. Indeed, we have recently been shocked by revelations about children battered by their parents, and now the studies of Richard Gelles show that a lot of violence also takes place between American husbands and wives and that by no means is all of it initiated by the husbands.

On the other hand, recent studies have made it clear that the outstanding characteristic of strong, healthy, happy families is that the members of those families freely express appreciation and affection for each other. This is really not very surprising; we all respond warmly to expressions of appreciation and affection.

Fortunately, we are gaining today a great deal of new insight into what we now call couple communication. Behavioral scientists have recently been studying this subject extensively and have brought to light new knowledge that we have never had before. Sherod Miller and his associates at the University of Minnesota have thoroughly investigated the complicated field of human communication, and have extracted from it much helpful material applicable to married couples. They have then taken out all the technical language and condensed it into a twelve-hour course that can be taught to a group of couples by a qualified instructor. This couple communication program is now spreading rapidly across North America. It is fully described in Miller's book *Alive and Aware,* which is listed in Appendix B of this book. We shall be using some of this material with you in one of your work units.

Another project for improving couple communication is the Conjugal Relationship Enhancement Program (CREP), developed at Pennsylvania State University by Bernard Guerney and his associates (see Appendix C under "Institute for the Development of Emotional and Life Skills"). Among other things, this course trains couples to listen to each other with "empathy," which means teaching them to identify with the feelings of another person. We are including an exercise for you that will let you try this out for yourselves.

There are also programs in "creative listening" now being developed in different parts of the country. We have no firsthand experience of these, but we keep hearing good reports from those who have been involved in them.

These new insights into effective communication have also been applied to parent-child relationships. Parent Effectiveness Training (P.E.T.), developed by psychologist Thomas Gordon, is being widely extended across the country; it is fully described in his book by the same title (see Appendix B). There exist several other similar programs.

Psychologists are also investigating what they call self-disclosure. Their studies show clearly that the way we develop effective intimate relationships is by opening up our inner selves to each other—not suddenly, but by a gradual mutual process of making ourselves vulnerable and developing trust. This is the basis of most deep, meaningful friendships, and it is the foundation of marriages that become affectionate and tender. Husband and wife can't really get close to each other as long as they keep up their defenses. They must learn to communicate at least some of their inner personal thoughts, feelings, and intentions. This creates a climate of mutual trust in which love, affection, and tenderness can grow.

We have already asked you to begin learning to do this in your daily dialogues, and we shall return to this subject later. The point we are making now is that effective communication is vital to the achievement of an effective marriage. The figures quoted in the study made by the Family Service Association of America leave no room for doubt on this point.

11
Getting in Touch with Each Other

The field of human communication, and even that of couple communication, becomes quite complex as you get deeply into it. We are not going to bother you here with these complexities. All we shall do is to summarize for you, as briefly and clearly as we can, what you need to understand and learn in order to acquire a set of new tools that you can use to make your marriage function better.

First, each of you will need to learn to get in touch with your own feeling states and to be aware of what is going on inside you. You can't communicate your feelings intelligently to another person unless you are ready to try to understand them yourself.

Lower animals have a set of emotions to which they respond instinctively, and which governs their behavior. Humans are endowed with very much the same emotional equipment; but we have the power, to a far greater extent, to adapt and change our behavior so as to make our lives pleasant and happy. Either our feelings control us—and often drive us in directions in which we don't really want to go—or *we* take over the control—just as the captain of a sailing ship can trim the sails to propel the boat in directions other than the one in which the wind happens to be blowing.

At the dinner table, a husband suddenly lashes out at his wife. Taken by surprise and hurt by his attack, she defends herself. They then get into a violent quarrel. When it's over, they hardly know what they were fighting about. It turns out that he had had a very difficult day at the office, where he was severely reprimanded by his boss. He thought this was quite unfair and had to stifle a strong urge to shout back, and even to punch the boss's nose. So he came home full of smoldering indignation, and it took only a mildly critical remark from his wife, which he misinterpreted, to make him explode.

If he had been fully aware of his raw emotional state, he would have explained his feelings to his wife when he got home. And if she had understood what was going on, she could have put her arm around him, comforted him, restored his bruised ego, and earned his loving gratitude. This is what we mean by being in touch with one's feelings and dealing with them purposefully.

This week, we're going to give you a daily exercise to help you get in touch with your feelings and to learn to look behind them and find out what is going on. We believe married couples should try to keep in continual touch with each other's feeling states. We have made a practice of doing this for years. We start off every day by checking on each other's feelings, and when we are reunited after being separated—even for a few hours—the first order of business, before passing on any items of news about what we have been doing, is to ask each other about our feeling states. So when we say, "How are you?" we really mean that we want to know, and that we expect a full answer.

Knowing the state of your partner's emotions prevents all sorts of misunderstandings and mistakes. There are things we can say to each other when we are cheerful that would be hurtful when we are depressed. There are actions that would push tolerance to the breaking point in a person tired or discouraged, that at other times he could accept or even enjoy. To live close to another person and not know the state of his or her emotions is like walking in a minefield—you could touch off an explosion at any moment.

So the first vitally important lesson to learn in couple communication is to be aware of your own feelings, whatever they are, and to keep your partner informed about them.

A second important skill for couples is to know how to complete their communication cycles. This is an elementary principle in communication theory; yet for many couples we have worked with, it has turned out to be a completely new idea. Let us explain it very simply.

The husband comes home and tells his wife that an old film classic is to be shown at the local movie theater next Wednesday evening—just that evening.

What is he really saying? He might just be passing on an interesting piece of information. In that case, his wife might reply, "Really? I suppose there are still some people who haven't seen that movie." There the conversation ends.

However, the husband may, at the back of his mind, have the idea that they might both go and see this film again; but he doesn't like to say this outright, because he knows that his wife has a class on Wednesday evenings. Or, he may know that she especially likes that film, and therefore he ought to tell her that it's on again; yet he hopes she won't ask *him* to go, because he has planned an outing with some men friends for that evening.

If the wife responds by treating his statement as a piece of information, he is going to be frustrated, satisfied, or relieved, according to what his purpose was in making the statement. And if the wife doesn't know what his purpose is, she has no way of knowing what reply to give. This is the way all kinds of misunderstandings occur in marriage, sometimes leading to hurt feelings and even to bitter quarrels.

Fortunately, there is a simple way to avoid any possibility of a misunderstanding. It isn't necessary to use it in most situations, but when the issue isn't clear, it can be a lifesaver. A couple who learn it and use it when necessary need never be caught in another misunderstanding.

Three simple steps are involved. First, the "sender" states his message. Second, the "receiver" summarizes what he thinks he heard (what we call feedback). Third, the sender can either confirm the feedback if it is right or correct it if it is wrong. When the cycle is completed, there can be no possible mistake. Airplane pilots have to do this because their lives may depend on it. Married couples would do well to learn it, because their happiness may depend on it.

Of course, we're not suggesting that you do this all the time. That would be an absurdly clumsy process—and usually unnecessary. But we think couples should practice completing communication cycles—and get used to it—so they can use this technique in any situation in which confusion is likely to arise or has already arisen. When in doubt, ask for feedback!

Another very useful tool in couple communication is "scoring your wants." There's a more technical name for it, but we won't bother you with that. Let's use an illustration.

John and Mary have planned to eat out together. John comes home with a splitting headache, but he knows how eager Mary was about their plan; so he cheerfully asks her if she is ready. Actually, she isn't now keen about it anymore, because she has discovered there's a TV program on that she doesn't want to miss. However, she doesn't want to disappoint John, so she goes upstairs to change her clothes. The dinner is a disaster, because neither of them wanted to go.

This would have been prevented if they had scored their wants. John would have said, "Ready, honey? Or shall we take our scores first?" The score is quite simple—how much do you really want this on a scale from zero to ten? Mary would have said, "I'm ready to go, but I am afraid my score is only three or four." John would have then replied, "OK, let's call it off tonight. My score is even lower than that."

The situation could get awkward, of course, when they both

scored five, or one scored four and the other six! But at least they know the facts, so that a sensible decision can be arrived at.

No discussion of couple communication can leave out the very sensitive question, "How much of ourselves ought we to share with each other? Should it be total self-disclosure?"

One simple answer is that it never can be. We don't *know* our total selves. There are depths in us that we are quite unable to reach or to express. In all of us, there is an inner self that can never be known to another. The German poet Rilke said that "even between the closest human beings, infinite distances continue to exist," but that "a wonderful living side-by-side can grow up, if they [human beings] succeed in loving the distance between them."

That doesn't really answer the question, however. We would definitely say that the married couple quite justifiably may, and in some cases must, withhold some communications from each other. This could apply in three kinds of situations.

First, the couple are not justified in disclosing information given them confidentially by other people outside the relationship. If they were to do this, they would be betraying a trust.

Second, they may not always be justified in making a full self-disclosure. Being honest about themselves to their marriage partner is in general a very important principle. But the ethic of honesty may clash with another principle that has an even higher priority—the ethic of love.

We have known couples who carried the principle of honesty to extreme lengths. They considered it to be an obligation to blurt out everything that occurred to them at the moment it occurred. One husband, while making love to his wife, confessed to her that he was having a fantasy about having intercourse with another woman who was a mutual friend. This is what is sometimes called being brutally frank, and brutality has no place in a loving relationship. Another husband confessed to his wife about an affair he had had outside the marriage, and after his confession he heaved a sigh of relief and said, "Now it's off my mind." In reply, his wife heaved a sigh of anguish and said, "That may be, but now it's on *my* mind!"

Third, and for the same reason as above, any criticism of your partner should always be made very sensitively and gently. A program prepared for couples to use at home, and designed to promote "marriage enrichment," asks them at one point to sit down together and tell everything they dislike about each other! This is emphatically *not* our conception of marriage enrichment. It could in fact wreck a marriage relationship beyond repair.

The Bible enjoins us to "speak the truth in love." Self-disclosure is the essence of a deep and meaningful relationship between husband and wife, but disclosures that might be painful either have to be made at the right time and in the right way or (occasionally) not at all. Love must always be sensitive enough to avoid inflicting needless pain.

12
What Style Are You In?

One of the most helpful insights that has come to us in the area of couple communication is the identification of the four communication styles. This is part of the couple communication course to which we have already referred. The University of Minnesota researchers have made it clear, however, that the identification of the four styles was not part of their original work. They borrowed this concept from W. F. Hill, a California psychologist, and to him must go a share of the credit for enriching a great many marriages.

We ourselves have found that identifying the four communication styles—and learning to use them properly—has greatly improved our sensitivity to each other. The description we give you here will be simplified, and we shall include in it some of our own interpretations.

Style I needs very little comment. It is much the most widely used mode of communication. It consists of passing on information—usually with very little emotion involved. This is the style we all use in most of our everyday conversations about events taking place around us—the friendly, sociable, chitchat that goes on all the time when people who know each other are together.

Style II is something else. It is the style in which you assert yourself and try to dominate or manipulate the other person.

Between marriage partners, it is used to blame, to demand, to control, to put down. You use it when you are trying to force the other person to change or to surrender. We all use it—some of us often. There are married couples who seem to use Style II most of the time. It can be used, too, in very subtle ways—for example, in persuading and advising, which are only thinly veiled forms of manipulation. It can be used (in the form of sarcasm) as what could be described as humor. Some people are even clever enough to pay what sound like compliments in Style II—for example, the husband who says to his wife, in a cynical tone, "You're a great mother, aren't you?"

We have described Style II as "the style with the sting in its tail." It carries a hidden barb, which the receiver of the message always feels. Indeed, we think that the receiver must always be the final judge of what has transpired. Even when the sender wasn't intending it to be Style II, if the receiver feels the sting, then it *is* Style II!

This style *can* have some practical uses, especially in its milder forms. But when it is used between husband and wife to deal with some issue in their relationship, it is invariably harmful and unproductive. We, as a married couple, are continually trying to give up using it altogether.

Style II tries to manipulate a person by hurting him. It invariably puts him on the defensive, and if persisted in, it produces a Style II response. This is how couples get into fights. One injects a sting into the other, and the recipient retaliates. We'll delve into this process more fully when we deal with anger in marriage.

Style III is the reasoning, diagnosing, analyzing style. It operates at the intellectual rather than emotional level. It is speculative, looking objectively at what is going on, seeking explanations and possible solutions. It is tentative and open-ended. It doesn't get anything done, but it can lead to decisions as to what *needs to be done.*

When couples are confronted by some difficulty or disagreement, what often happens is that one goes into Style II, that is, blaming and attacking the other. This causes the other to respond, also in Style II, and soon they are arguing or fighting. This gets them nowhere, and they may simply give up trying to find a solution. Many marriages have a heavy backlog of unresolved disagreements that recur from time to time, cause a fight, and are put back on the heap still unresolved. A marriage in this condition is in a continuing state of suppressed tension and is by no means a pleasant emotional climate to live in.

However, the couple may face the fact that they don't want to go on living in this way; they may try to find a solution by moving to Style III. The usual opening gambit is: "Let's be *reasonable*. We're behaving like kids. Let's act like adults and try to figure out what's going on." So they begin to analyze the situation—what's happening here, why do I do this, and why do you do that? The hope is that an intellectual understanding will tidy things up.

Unfortunately, this seldom happens, and the couple, having made this great effort to deal with their difficulty on a higher level, feel defeated and discouraged. *Why* doesn't it work?— because what they have done is to try to deal with the issue *apart from the feelings involved.* They have said: "Let's leave our ugly feelings down there, move up to this more elevated rational level, and get it all straightened out." But *the feelings are a basic part of the issue, and they can't settle it by leaving them out.* Yet, they can't be cool and rational with angry, destructive emotions simmering just beneath the surface. So it seems quite hopeless, and many couples give up in despair.

At this point, witness the dramatic entry of Style IV, which provides the answer! All couples are familiar with the first three styles. But for most, Style IV is a completely new concept. It has very little place in our biological heritage, which teaches us to grab what we want and to oppose anyone who gets in our way, or in our cultural heritage, which teaches us to base all our actions on reason. Style IV takes us into a new dimension—that of the shared life in which our individual happiness comes only through shared happiness, and where we make ourselves vulnerable in order to achieve intimacy with another person whom we love and trust. Since this is the goal of the companionship marriage, Style IV brings a flood of new light and hope to struggling, discouraged couples.

In Style IV, you share with your partner whatever feelings you have honestly and openly. You say: "Here's what I'm feeling right now. This is where I am." But that isn't all. There are two vitally important conditions: (1) that you do this without blaming or attacking your partner (2) that you do it without defending yourself.

Obviously, this is not easy to do. It certainly doesn't come naturally. When you're confronting someone else with whom you have a difference of opinion or who is frustrating you, it seems crazy to take down all your defenses and open yourself up to attack. We might, on that account alone, dismiss using Style IV as a suggestion unworthy of consideration. But we can't do that—for the simple reason that it works! Again and again, it is effective where everything else fails.

Suppose your partner approaches you in Style II. You feel blamed, manipulated, attacked, demeaned. What is your natural response?—to clench your fists, tense your muscles, defend yourself, fight back.

But suppose your partner comes to you in Style IV, saying: "I'm in trouble. I feel put down and demeaned, and I'm struggling with hurt feelings. I *could* put all the blame on you, but I refuse to do that. It's your understanding and help I need. The fault isn't yours. The trouble is that our relationship isn't working right, and I wish we could do something about it. Won't you help me to get it all straightened out?" How would you react to this? You're not being attacked. You're being appealed to. It's an invitation to get behind the unpleasant things that are going on between you and to clear up the source of the bad feelings.

We said there is little of Style IV in our biological heritage. However, this is not entirely true. Animals of the same species,

86

when they confront each other in wrath, occasionally use this style. One decides that he just doesn't *want* to fight. He drops his guard, lets down his defenses—even exposes his jugular vein! When this happens, we are told that the opponent doesn't take advantage and move in for the kill. The fight is called off.

In our own experience, and in that of other couples who have taken this seriously, it really does work. Not always at first, though. We can recall a wife who went home and tried Style IV on her husband, then complained to us later that he had simply ridiculed her. What became clear was that he had become so accustomed to her use of Style II that when she suddenly changed her tactics, he suspected she had cooked up some subtle new weapon to hit him with. When she tried to explain, it was all so much out of keeping with her normal attitude that he treated her efforts as a joke and teased her unmercifully. No one can promise that Style IV will always work—at least not until husband and wife enter together into a commitment to adopt it without reservations. But what we *can* say is that where Style IV doesn't work, nothing else will. There is no Style V!

We need to add that Style IV by itself is not enough. It is an *invitation* to work on the issue. If the invitation is accepted, the couple can then move to Style III and find out together what unhealthy things are going on and how they can be cleared up. This is quite different from moving from Style II to Style III and leaving the feelings behind. When we move from Style IV, we can *take our feelings with us* for full investigation, because we are not using them destructively to tear each other down. And, because they are not aggressive feelings, they can provide the necessary motivation for action and change. So using Style IV and Style III together provides the winning combination.

For us, the discovery of Style IV was not altogether new. When we learned about it, we recognized an old friend. We had discovered it in the course of our long quest for an effective way of dealing with anger in our relationship. What the couple communication program did for us was to define more clearly

87

the nature and scope of Style IV, as well as its relationship to the other three styles.

As we see it, any couple dedicated to the quest for a really happy marriage should understand the four styles and learn to identify and use them wisely. For us, this has meant an agreement to try to give up entirely the use of Style II in dealing with issues that arise in our relationship. If either of us feels the sting in a statement from the other, it is our policy to challenge it at once by saying, usually in a good-humored fashion, "Sorry, I can't accept that message. I think it's Style II. What do you think?" If the sender of the message agrees, then the message is canceled, and another approach is used.

13
Work Units for Third and Fourth Weeks

Our purpose for these next two weeks is quite clear. We want you to focus on your communication system—to examine it, to find out where it needs improvement, to try out some new approaches, and to adopt those that promise to be helpful. Unless you are one of those rare couples who already have a highly efficient and smoothly operating communication system, we can promise that if you work diligently at the assignments we are giving you, you are going to make some gratifying progress.

You have already been making some preliminary experiments in communication—the exercises you have done, as well as the daily dialogues, involved you in the sharing of thoughts and feelings and challenged you to greater openness toward each other. But in these units we shall go much further, offering you a whole set of tools that you can use to grow together.

Schedule for Third Week

Preparation: Read or reread chapters 10, 11, and 12. Also, go over the Ten and Ten reflections of the past week.

Saturday: Two-hour session
              First hour (H leads)—Evaluation exercise on
              communication
              Second hour (W leads)—Discussion of Ten
              and Ten reflections

Sunday to
Friday: Evaluation of feelings (H and W lead alternate
              days.)

Directions

The first hour of your two-hour session should be spent doing, and then sharing, another evaluation exercise. This resembles the exercise you did two weeks ago, but the focus is entirely on your communication system.

Here's what to do. In your notebook, write down the following:

1. Three to five areas of your relationship about which you think you communicate well. You are both able to say freely and comfortably all that needs to be said. You can hear and understand each other. You can talk together and reach conclusions with hardly any chance of misunderstanding.
2. Three to five areas of your relationship about which you communicate poorly. You don't get through to each other clearly, and you have difficulty facing and resolving the issues.
3. Any areas of your relationship about which you can't communicate at all, or get into very seldom or so superficially that you don't achieve any real understanding or make any progress.

Take about fifteen minutes to work at this. Then, for the rest of the first hour, share with each other what you have written— section by section. See how far your evaluations agree. Look at differences in the way you see your communication system. Consider what you have learned from this exercise.

In the second hour, we want you again to go back over your daily Ten and Ten dialogues of the past week. What you were doing then was to try to look at your thoughts and feelings about the marriage and to share them with each other. In the light of what you have now learned in reading chapters 10, 11, and 12, how well were you understanding each other in those daily dialogues? How honest were you able to be about yourselves? How comfortably could you accept each other's reflections? How openly were you able to share your inner thoughts and feelings? You will be resuming the Ten and Ten dialogues later, after a two-week break. We want you at this point to evaluate your early efforts, then to come back to the experience with new insights.

Instead of the daily dialogue, this week we want you to make a careful investigation of your *feelings.* Look at them alone in your personal ten minutes each day, then share your reflections in your time together. One way would be to take a particular emotional state each day, which would allow you to look at six in all. Enter your reflections in your notebook, and ask yourself:

1. When I have this particular feeling, how does it affect me? How do I deal with it? How free am I to share it with my partner?
2. What kinds of situations produce this feeling in me? When I get this feeling, what's likely to be the cause of it?
3. How can I deal with this feeling?—that is, how can I express it creatively if it is positive or use it constructively if it is negative? How can my marriage partner share this feeling with me or help me to handle it?

For your use in this exercise, here's a list of common feeling-states that people experience. Out of the twenty-four we have given you here, you can pick six or more to examine this week. Select ones that you really want to explore. Positive and negative feelings alternate on the list, and you can pick some of each.

Pleased — Anxious — Hopeful — Lonely — Proud — Insecure — Excited — Sad — Contented — Angry — Confident — Bored — Grateful — Scared — Affectionate — Frustrated — Sexy — Depressed — Eager — Foolish — Elated — Confused — Calm — Apathetic.

In the exercise, you should reflect not only upon how you yourself react to having these feelings but also upon how you react when you become aware of them in your partner.

The purpose of the exercise is to help you to become more aware of your feelings, to deal appropriately with them, and to be comfortable about sharing them with each other. Married couples who can't be open to each other's feelings may be physically close, but emotionally they are living a long way apart.

Schedule for Fourth Week

Preparation: Reread chapters 10, 11, and 12.

Saturday: Two-hour session
First hour (W leads)—Practice the four communication styles.
Second hour (H leads)—Discuss evaluation-of-feelings exercise done during past week.

Sunday to
Friday: Daily—Practice responsive listening.

Directions

For your first hour on Saturday, go through the communication styles together, and be sure you can identify each of them clearly. You need not spend much time on Style I, but practice the others by talking about one or two "touchy" issues in your relationship—issues that quickly stir up strong feelings.

Take each of these issues in turn, and let one of you deliberately lead off using Style II. Don't exaggerate or dramatize

92

this; just speak as you normally do when you are frustrated or annoyed. If you normally don't express yourself angrily, let your hostile feelings come out as part of the exercise, so that you and your partner can experience how you sound in this role. Then, let the one being treated to Style II identify the sting by explaining exactly how it felt and what kinds of feelings it stirred up in response.

Now switch, and using the same situation, try to approach your partner about it in Style IV. If you haven't done this before, you might find it quite difficult at first—this is an entirely new experience for many people. The goal is to share your feelings openly and honestly—without attacking your partner and without defending yourself. Keep working at it, and encourage your partner to help you by trying to respond positively when you really do it right.

Finally, move into Style III, discussing the issue *and the feelings involved* calmly and objectively, and trying to work out a plan to neutralize the situation through mutual understanding and cooperation.

When one partner has had a turn at trying the three styles, let the other partner do the same. Cover as many issues as the time allows.

Follow up this exercise in your normal everyday conversations by checking on your styles from time to time. You might say, for example: "What style am I in now?" "Aren't you getting into Style II?" or "I guess this is a situation where I ought to use Style IV. Let me have a try—but I may need your help." or "Why don't we see whether we can handle this in Style III?" Get used to knowing, at any given time, what styles you are using. Once a couple really get sensitized to the unproductive nature of Style II, they will want to give it up as a way of trying to resolve their differences.

For your second hour, we suggest that you go back over the evaluations of your feelings you have been working on in your daily dialogues this past week and try to summarize what you have learned about accurately analyzing your emotional states (positive and negative) and about communicating them to each other and helping each other to deal with them.

Your daily dialogue this week will be spent in responsive listening. This is an exercise that uses the communication cycle to enable a person to find out how effectively he can be an empathic listener and how accurately he can give another person feedback. You will need a watch or clock with a second hand or, better still, a timer. An oven timer will do nicely.

When your turn comes, you should have chosen a situation in your relationship about which you personally sometimes find it difficult to get an effective response from the other—for example—your concern about practicing economy or your difficulty in hurrying or your sense of not being taken seriously.

Now take turns, and time everything closely. The one who begins has five minutes (no more, no less) to present his or her situation as clearly as possible—*without interruption*. The other simply listens, without even making a gesture that could be interpreted as a response. When time is up, the watch or timer is handed to the partner who has been speaking, who now takes over as timekeeper. A period of two minutes is allowed for silent reflection (don't look at each other or make gestures); then the partner who has so far been listening has three minutes (again without interruption) to give feedback ("Here's what I think I heard you saying"). After this feedback, allow another two minutes for reflection; then give the first speaker three minutes to evaluate the feedback, indicating what has been correctly heard, what has not been correctly heard, and anything that seems not to have been heard at all. The final five minutes may be used by both of you to discuss the exercise and the way you both reacted to it.

This probably all sounds very mechanical. But never mind; do it all the same. It should teach you a lot about responsive listening and about completing a communication cycle. It should also enable you to judge how well you can use empathy, which is the ability to see a situation through the eyes of another or, as we sometimes say, to stand in another person's shoes. Obviously, this is a very important skill to develop in marriage. Husbands and wives often complain, "I don't think my partner really understands how I feel."

PART IV
Resolving Conflicts Creatively

14
Never Waste a Good Conflict

"And so they were married, and lived happily ever after."

This blissful fairy-tale picture of the handsome prince and the despised kitchen maid, united at last after many hardships and adventures and finally entering a matrimonial haven of unending romance, has delighted generations of ecstatic children. And it has wrought untold havoc among those very same children when, years later, they themselves went forth from their wedding ceremonies to face hazards of which they had received no warning and for which they had been given no preparation.

Nobody likes to discredit age-old legends. But we have to be realistic. Let us follow the prince and his bride beyond the point at which the fairy tales conveniently leave off.

We will discreetly pass over the wedding night. At breakfast next morning, a minor crisis occurred when the bride saw irritation wrinkle her husband's brow as he became aware of her incredible lack of table manners. Later in the day, his sophisticated talk about subjects she had never even heard of threw her into a state of near panic. In the days that followed, the prince was frequently embarrassed by the titters of the courtiers at his bride's awkward antics, while she found the mincing manners of the nobility utterly alien to all her concepts of good behavior. Other differences between them steadily accumulated, and their private attempts to resolve their disagreements soon led to harsh words and bitter tears. The prince tried unsuccessfully to fight back deep misgivings about what he had done by marrying this clumsy girl who just didn't know how to behave in public, while she began to feel desperately lonely in the alien atmosphere of the court and to entertain secret longings to escape from it all and regain the comfortable security of her kitchen. Here we are only discussing obvious cultural differences between them. Concerning differences of temperament, of personal preference, and of value orientation, we can't even begin to guess—but these certainly existed, and some of them were probably wide and deep.

A modern writer has even suggested that marriage has traditionally been a cultural confidence game, holding out dazzling rewards to entice the innocent victims into a trap, which then snaps shut and lands them in misery. This explanation obviously represents a jaundiced viewpoint, but it is not entirely a gross misrepresentation.

Why are we saying all this?—because there can be no way to a happy marriage unless the truth is faced. And the truth is that our culture has cruelly deceived us by suggesting that any marriage can possibly be free from conflicts. On the contrary, conflict is an inevitable, integral, and inescapable part of the marriage relationship. Until we accept that, and begin to put our conflicts to creative use, our chances of ever achieving enduring love in marriage are slim indeed. Unless we face our conflicts realistically, and resolve them, true happiness in marriage will only last as long as we can go on kidding ourselves that the conflicts don't exist, and continue pushing them out of sight. And for many marriages, that won't be very long.

We may seem to be going out of our way to make startling and even alarming statements. We want to assure you that we are speaking to you very earnestly. We are also speaking out of a long and extensive experience of seeing marriages from the inside—marriages in serious trouble over a period of forty years and so-called good marriages over a period of fourteen years. We have developed our views about marital conflict, not out of theoretical speculation, but out of personal experience in our own relationship and out of close observation of thousands of other marriages.

First, let us try to explain what conflict in marriage is all about. This is so important that we want to use a diagram, adapted from one in our earlier book *We Can Have Better Marriages—If We Really Want Them* (see Appendix B for details).

The diagram shows the husband and wife at some distance from each other. When they first meet, they are of course comparative strangers. Obviously, they have some similarities, otherwise, they would not have been drawn together. But between them are also a great many differences. If we were to ask you, as a married couple, to sit down and make a complete list of the differences between you—physical, mental, emotional, spiritual, and all the rest—you would never finish the task. The list would just go on and on and on.

What's wrong with differences? Some are positively helpful. Studies of mate selection show that people are attracted to each other both by their similarities and their differences. The theory of complementarity suggests that in choosing our marriage partners we are attracted by qualities in another person that are lacking in ourselves; in other words, we hope, either by assimilation or by association, to gain these qualities for the enhancement of our own personalities.

But notice something else. Differences between people can seem very attractive at a distance, but these same attractive qualities in another person can become quite irritating when the couple enter into a shared life. Boy meets girl. Boy likes to spend his vacations climbing in the mountains. Girl likes to go to the shore. After their separate vacations, they find it stimulating and exciting to hear from each other—what he did in the mountains,

101

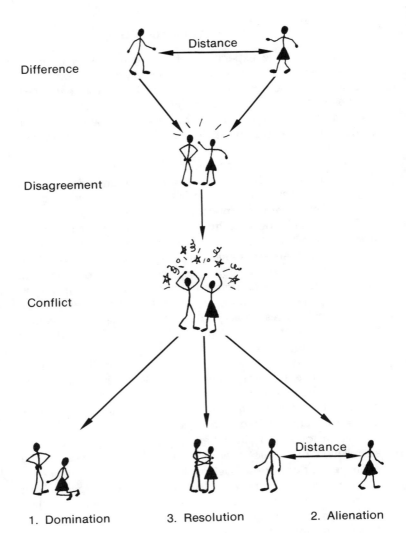

Difference

Distance

Disagreement

Conflict

1. Domination   3. Resolution   2. Alienation

Distance

Diagram 1
Conflict Resolution

what she did at the shore. But then they marry, and they want to go on vacation together. Where do they go? To the mountains? To the shore? Half the time to each? Or do they go to neither? When you begin to get close to someone and share that person's life, differences that have been interesting and even exciting can turn into disagreements and cause trouble. When we begin to seek intimacy, we can get in each other's way and block each other's living space.

On the diagram, we can see this happening. Husband and wife move closer to each other; disagreement arises, and a few sparks begin to fly. However, loving people can tolerate a certain amount of disagreement—for a while. They can persuade themselves that it's just a temporary disturbance and will soon go away.

As we try to mesh our lives together more closely, though, we find that the disagreements don't go away. As husband and wife struggle to resolve their disagreements, the sparks fly thick and fast. Disagreements heat up and become conflict. That's exactly what conflict is—disagreement heated up. We are all familiar with the hot emotions—irritation, frustration, exasperation, hostility—in a word, anger. And the harder we try to face our conflicts, the hotter the emotions tend to become.

So now we face a crisis. We want closeness and intimacy, because love impels us to share our lives more and more deeply. But we find ourselves cheated. Instead of deeper love, we find our love blotted out by anger. You can't be loving and angry at the same time. We want to love each other, and instead we find ourselves hating each other. And the more we try to work through the conflict, the more anger is generated, and the more painful the situation becomes.

All married couples understand this experience. We call it the love-anger cycle. When we explain it to a group of couples, they nod their heads. They know exactly what we mean; they've been there.

Go back for a minute to where we started. Our culture doesn't prepare us for marital conflicts. We're supposed to live happily ever after. Conflict in marriage is portrayed as something evil, something sinister, like the serpent that raises its ugly head in the Garden of Eden, threatening to destroy our happiness. "Nice" couples never admit that they have conflicts, though most of them do. They have been taught that it is shameful even to disagree, let alone to fight. So they keep the secret, and the widening deception goes on.

All right, what do you do when you are in the thick of conflict in your marriage and this conflict isn't supposed to happen? Go back to diagram 1, and you will see that there are three possible ways of dealing with the situation. Unfortunately, most of us don't choose the right one.

The first way is the one chosen by practically all marriages in the past. In the old days, and in the older cultures, marriages had to be stable whether they were happy or not. So, to avoid conflict altogether, the husband-wife relationship was structured as a one-vote system. By arranging for the husband to be dominant and the wife to be submissive, disagreement was conveniently avoided. Consequently, intense conflicts were not likely to arise. The diagram portrays this situation on the left, as the first type of solution—domination by one partner. Although the dominant partner was traditionally the husband, there are marriages today in which conflict is avoided by the wife becoming dominant.

The second type of solution is the one commonly resorted to in large numbers of modern marriages. The couples concerned are committed to the companionship type of marriage, which involves a two-vote system. But two-vote systems are very difficult to operate. The conflict cannot be resolved, because the underlying disagreement makes husband and wife both unwilling to give ground, and the resulting clash of conficting wills produces mounting tension and considerable anger. This becomes so painful that it is finally intolerable, and the partners retreat into distance and progressive alienation from each other.

Conflicts are not resolved, but peace (of a sort) is established. What the partners often don't realize, however, is that this way of handling conflict means the abandonment of any hopes they had of intimacy and a loving, tender relationship. Millions of our marriages today take this course, the partners gradually drifting apart and becoming less and less involved in each other's lives, until the relationship is an empty shell.

Now look at the third type of solution, in the center of the diagram. The couples who give up and miss out don't realize that the happiness they were seeking is really there, but that it can be realized only when they work right through the conflict, instead of evading it. If they only knew how to do this to the point of resolution, they would strengthen their relationship instead of weakening it. But they don't know this, because the culture doesn't tell them that the conflicts in a marriage are really the growth points in the relationship, and that the creative use of conflict is the golden key that opens the door to lasting happiness.

Let's say all this just a little differently by using another diagram, which is used in various forms by psychologists. We need to introduce you also to the term they use. Fortunately it isn't an obscure term. It's the simple word *pinch.*

Everyone knows what a pinch is—a sudden, sharp, painful, and usually unexpected pressure on a sensitive part of your anatomy that makes you want to recoil and move away. We usually talk about a *physical* experience. But this time, we're talking about an *emotional* pinch, an experience caused by some disturbing word or action on the part of another person that makes you want to draw away and disengage from the person concerned. Experiences of this kind occur occasionally in all relationships, even in the best relationships.

There are two versions of the diagram. In both, husband and wife begin by moving toward each other, seeking intimacy. As they get closer, they become involved in disagreements that can easily heat up into conflicts (you'll remember this on the earlier

105

diagram). The first couple we are now considering are enlightened about the use of conflict. So, as soon as one feels a pinch, he or she faces it honestly and shares its cause with the other (using Style IV, of course!). At the onset of the pinch, the one who feels the hurt instinctively backs away from the other; but as the issue is honestly faced and resolved between them, a warm feeling of trust replaces the feeling of revulsion the pinch caused, and they now both move a little closer. As this is repeated over and over in a series of pinches, each conflict is faced and dealt with as it arises. The result is that the couple find in time that their disagreements cease to threaten them, because they know they can be handled and resolved. So they are able to settle for a continuing close relationship. In the diagram, the pinches are shown as arrows pointing inward, meaning that the pinches are used to draw the couple toward each other and not away from each other.

After the critical adjustment period is over, a couple will of course still have occasional pinches; but since they always share and resolve them, their relationship of intimacy is not disturbed. The diagram shows these continuing pinches, at less frequent intervals, still being used to preserve intimacy. Each potential conflict is treated as a growth point; it is used to strengthen the relationship.

Now look at the second version of the diagram. This couple also want to move closer to each other. But when a pinch comes, and the one who is hurt backs away, they are unable to deal with it. The one who feels the pinch just doesn't say anything, or he or she tries to discuss it and gets a negative reaction. So the process of avoiding a developing conflict becomes a habit, and each pinch now helps to push the couple further and further apart. In time, they will reach a safe distance from which further pinches won't bother them anymore. But in the process, they will have given up their hope of achieving intimacy. At best, they can live together in mutual tolerance; at worst, they will drift progressively apart until the relationship becomes completely superficial.

Sherod Miller and his associates at the University of Minnesota explain that when a couple have the insight and skill to see their conflicts as potentially creative, they can turn a pinch into a growth point. If they don't have this skill, each pinch is likely to become a disruption point. Therefore, every pinch that develops in their relationship is in reality a "choice point." In making this choice, over and over again, the couples themselves, whether they know it or not, are deciding for or against an intimate, loving relationship.

We should add, as a note of hope and encouragement, that a couple represented by the second version of the diagram can at

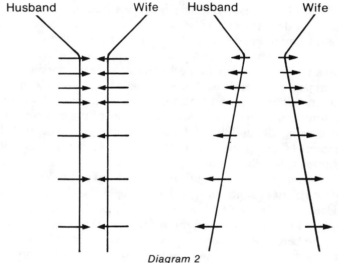

Diagram 2
Intimacy Sustained or Destroyed
by Resolving or Avoiding Conflict

any time agree to change their policy, make a different adjustment, and eventually learn to use conflict creatively.

So, as we said in the title of this chapter, never waste a good conflict!

15
How to Deal with Anger

An old Indian legend tells how Twashtri, the Creator, ran into some difficulties when he provided the Hindu equivalent of Adam with the Hindu equivalent of Eve. Here is the story.

"In the beginning, when Twashtri came to the creation of woman, he found that he had exhausted his materials in the making of man, and that no solid elements were left. In this dilemma, after profound meditation, he did as follows. He took the rotundity of the moon, and the curves of the creepers, and the clinging of tendrils, and the trembling of grass, and the slenderness of the reed, and the bloom of flowers, and the lightness of leaves, and the tapering of the elephant's trunk, and the glances of deer, and the clustering of rows of bees, and the joyous gaiety of sunbeams, and the weeping of clouds, and the fickleness of the winds, and the timidity of the hare, and the vanity of the peacock, and the softness of the parrot's bosom, and the hardness of adamant, and the sweetness of honey, and the cruelty of the tiger, and the warm glow of the fire, and the coldness of snow, and the chattering of jays, and the cooing of the Kokila, and the hypocrisy of the crane, and the fidelity of the chakrawaka; and compounding all these together he made woman, and gave her to man.

"But after one week, man came to him and said: 'Lord, this creature that you have given me makes my life miserable. She chatters incessantly, and teases beyond endurance, never leaving me alone: and she requires incessant attention, and takes all my time up, and cries about nothing and is always idle: and so I have come to give her back again as I cannot live with her.' So Twashtri said: 'Very well.' And he took her back. Then after another week, man came again to him and said: 'Lord, I find that my life is very lonely since I gave you back that creature. I remember how she used to dance and sing to me, and play with me, and cling to me; and her laughter was music, and she was beautiful to look at, and soft to touch: so give her back to me again.' So Twashtri said: 'Very well.' And he gave her back again.

"Then after only three days, man came back to him again, and said: 'Lord, I know not how it is: but after all, I have come to the conclusion that she is more of a trouble than a pleasure to me: so please take her back again.' But Twashtri said: 'Out on you! Be off! I will have no more of this. You must manage how you can.' The man said: 'But I cannot live with her.' And Twashtri replied: 'Neither could you live without her.' And he turned his back on man, and went on with his work. Then man said: 'What is to be done? For I cannot live either with her or without her.'"

The story as it stands, coming from an ancient culture based on male supremacy, makes woman out to be a troublesome creature. But with only a slight corrective twist, it becomes a vivid dramatization of the nature of marriage. Husband and wife *want* to be close, loving, and intimate—but in the process of sharing their lives, they activate disagreements that lead to conflict. So there they are, caught on the horns of a dilemma. We suspect that the poignancy of the man's despairing cry—"What is to be done? For I cannot live either with her or without her!"—lifts the curtain on a human drama that is as old as time.

The answer, obviously and logically, is the one we are presenting here. The couple must work through their conflicts and resolve them. Another way of approaching this is to say that the couple must go through a process of mutual adaptation, so that they can cooperate smoothly in a loving relationship that promotes individual and relational growth. For most people, the achievement of such harmony represents a high peak of human happiness. To love and to be loved—this surely is what brings emotional security and fulfills our deepest need for identity and a satisfying self-image. Havelock Ellis summed it up when he said, "To live is to love, and to love is to live."

All right, what prevents us from working through our conflicts? We have seen the answer quite clearly. It is the anger that is spontaneously developed when inevitable disagreements between us, caused by the clashes of our personalities or experiences, heat up. If we could only deal with the anger, and take it out of the picture, the way would then be open for the resolution of our conflicts.

We ourselves have come to the conclusion that this brings us to the root of the matter. We aren't saying that the resolution of conflict is easy, by any means. But we are convinced that resolution is possible when it is seen by both partners to be in their best interests.

That is all very well in theory, however. In real life, anger simply stands in the way, blocking every attempt of the couple to come together in a harmonious relationship. Conflict is like a ticking bomb that threatens to explode before it can be dismantled. The high explosive is anger. How can we defuse the bomb?

Over a number of years, we have given much thought to this question. We have done so because for a long time anger prevented us from developing the potential in our relationship, and we are now convinced that this is the great barrier standing in the way of nearly all couples who are striving to achieve healthy, growing marriages.

So we have sought to understand both the role of anger and the best ways of dealing with it. We have come to some conclusions that seem important, for they work for us and for other couples with whom we have shared them. We will try now to summarize those conclusions for your guidance.

What *is* anger? We all know it as a powerful feeling that takes hold of us under certain circumstances—usually when we are hurt or frustrated. When we study the physiology of anger, we find that a whole series of bodily changes take place: the heartbeat speeds up, adrenalinlike substances pour into the bloodstream, our muscles become tense, anticoagulants in the blood diminish, and much more. What does all this mean?

Anger is really a survival kit with which we are all endowed. These physical changes all have one clear purpose. They give us an immediate surge of extra energy so that we can deal with an emergency—either by fighting the enemy that threatens us or by running away faster than we have ever run before.

In the life of the jungle, what triggered this outpouring of energy was fear. Most creatures of the wild live in constant danger, so fear instantly prepares them for either fight or flight. But there are other situations in which survival may be threatened. Food that seems to be inaccessible may threaten starvation, and as frustration builds up, anger provides the extra energy to jump the gap or break through the obstacle.

In the comparative safety of civilized life, threats to survival don't often occur. The possibility of frustration is greatly increased, however. The higher our expectations, and the more numerous our needs, the more often will we find ourselves blocked. So anger in civilized man is much more often aroused by frustration than by fear. People differ greatly in the amount of frustration they can tolerate, but all of us have a flash point at which we experience a surge of anger. In marriage, as we have seen, this can easily happen, because we find ourselves in a situation in which expectations are high, and frustration can often occur. We would venture the opinion that for normal people, being married probably generates more anger than any other interpersonal situation in which they normally find themselves.

111

Now let us look more closely at what happens when we get angry. First, we must recognize that anger is a normal, healthy emotion with an important purpose in our lives. A person who doesn't get angry is not a normal human being. There is no need to be ashamed or guilty about anger. It provides the driving force to get many things done that need to be done.

Anyway, we achieve nothing by being ashamed of our anger, because we are not actually responsible for its onset. Anger develops spontaneously as a response to a stimulus—usually a stimulus outside ourselves. There just isn't time for us to decide whether or not to be angry; for our own protection, therefore, the initial surge of feeling, with its accompanying physical changes, is quite outside our control.

Once the anger is there, however, we *are* responsible for what we do about it. We must exercise our intelligence in the use of this surge of vital energy—fight with proper cunning and skill or run away by the best escape route. By the time we become aware of our anger, therefore, we have the power to control it. People who say they have an "uncontrollable" temper are deceiving themselves. They *allow* themselves to stamp and rage because at some time in the past (and perhaps still in the present) temper tantrums enabled them to get what they wanted.

Another common misunderstanding is the idea that by venting anger we get rid of it. The opposite is true. Venting anger sends a message to the body to continue the supply. Recent studies of the family by Murray Straus have shown that individuals who vent their anger tend, over time, to produce more and more anger and to vent it more and more vigorously until they finally resort to physical violence. To vent anger certainly releases the tensed-up muscles, and that brings a sense of physical relief. But venting anger almost invariably gets the other person angry too, and then you are going to need more and more anger to continue the fight.

Most of us know of only two ways to deal with our anger—vent it or suppress it. Because we have the power to control anger, we can train ourselves to bottle it up. Some people learn to do this habitually. But they don't get rid of their anger; it still simmers within them and has a poisonous effect. As long as the cause of the anger is still there, the state of anger tends to be maintained. Wanting to vent anger and not doing so creates an inner conflict.

However, when the cause of the anger is removed or recognized not to be the threat it seems to be, the state of anger quickly subsides. The bodily tension dies away, and our physical condition quickly returns to normal. This happens, for example, when anger is simulated by a false alarm. It also happens when we decide vented anger would be an inappropriate response— for example, if you discovered that you had misinterpreted what looked like a threatening attitude in your spouse. We have some power to decide when anger is inappropriate; and when we do, it subsides very quickly.

Now let us put all this together. Out of it we have developed a policy for our marriage, and you might like to consider trying it. We call it our Three-Step System. We had to make a contract that we would help each other put it into operation. At first, this was difficult, but now, it seldom fails.

Step One. We agree to *acknowledge* our anger to each other as soon as we become aware of it. This allows it no time to build up. We accept without question our right to be angry with each other, so no shame or guilt is implied by acknowledging it. And acknowledging anger is *not* venting it; it is simply communicating to the other person the state of our emotion, without accusation or blame.

Step Two. We *renounce* the right to vent anger on each other. We have come to the conclusion that anger is never appropriate in a love relationship. It's too damaging to our love, and there is always a better way to deal with it. So one of us will say to the other, "I'm getting angry with you, but you know that I'm not going to attack you." This means that the other partner doesn't

113

need to go on the defensive, which would result in retaliatory anger and be likely to lead to a fight.

Step Three. We *ask* for the other's help in dealing with the anger that has developed. This may seem a very odd way to go about it. But it works. If your partner is angry with you, and appeals to you to help clear it up, it is very much in your interest to respond. None of us likes being either the subject or the object of anger, but a coalition between subject and object proves to be unbeatable.

Our contract commits us to working on each anger situation that develops between us until we clear it up. Sometimes it is too hot to handle at once, but we make sure that we get to it with the least possible delay.

When we begin to work on an anger situation, we invariably arrive at one of two conclusions. In some situations, it turns out that the anger was unjustified, having been based on a misunderstanding of the other's motives or actions. In other situations, the anger *was* justified, because the provoked partner had been pushed by the other beyond the limits of his or her tolerance. In either case, an apology is appropriate on one side or the other.

But what is so gratifying is that as each situation is cleared up, we have the opportunity to learn more and more about possible anger-producing actions that can occur between us. So we gain the power, based on accurate knowledge, to avoid major crises. As we write this, for example, only two such crises have occurred in our relationship during the past year, and both were quite easily cleared up.

We don't claim that we have solutions for everyone—only for ourselves. There are some who believe in marital fighting Frankly, we don't. We believe that true intimacy in marriage is a state in which we can be defenseless and vulnerable with each other, and this is not possible if we have to be ready to go on guard against an attack at any moment.

Our hope is that by sharing our experience and our

conclusions with you, we may be able to help you to find your own way of defusing the anger bomb.

Once a married couple have freed themselves from any threat that anger could damage their relationship, their love is free to grow without hindrance. You can't be loving when you are angry, and you can't be angry when you're loving—the two exclude each other. But you can't be continuously loving, either, when the threat of possible anger hangs over you—however remote the threat may be. Only when you have brought anger completely under control in your marriage—and we mean by accepting and resolving it together, not by suppressing it—does the way lie clear and open to a continuing growth in love and intimacy.

16

Settling Disagreements by Negotiation

You may have been surprised by the fact that in our program for the improvement of your marriage we started you off with a bargaining session. We all know about bargaining, but we don't normally associate this with love and marriage. The word *bargaining* conjures up images of dickering in oriental bazaars and horse trading at country fairs. It seems to have more to do with settling strikes than with building marriages.

Yet bargaining plays a vital role in all transactions between human beings. Before money was ever invented, people got what they needed by barter, a process in which they reached agreement about the exchange of goods. You and I exchange a chicken for a basket of peaches, and we both go home satisfied. Of course we now use money to barter, but that doesn't change the process. We pay the grocer for our groceries, and he uses our money to pay his rent or to send his daughter to college.

Nowadays we use the word *negotiation* for *barter;* but what we do isn't any different. From settling an international dispute that might end in war, to reaching agreement on a labor contract to prevent a strike, to resolving a disagreement in marriage, we make use of exactly the same process of exchange.

You may reply that in marriage we don't use coercion as a weapon to get our way. Are you sure? We bribe and punish each other in all sorts of subtle ways. A husband may withhold money; a wife may withhold sex. A wife may nag to wear down her husband's resistance; a husband may act grouchy to compel his wife to give in. All this subtle, shady use of indulgence on the one hand, and deprivation on the other, is a basic ingredient in the games married couples play with each other.

What we recommend is that we bring our bargaining out into the open, recognize that it is an entirely respectable part of marriage, and do it aboveboard in a forthright and cooperative spirit. It represents a vital element in bringing about the growth and change that achieve a happy marriage, so let's look at it in that light. Let each of us, openly and honestly, say what we personally want and need. Then, let's see how we can best reconcile our differences.

The goal is equity, which means a fair share for each—a fair share of the goodies and of the chores. Much is being said these days about equality in marriage. We think the word *equity* is much better. *Equality* is, after all, a mathematical term, and it can only be justly applied when quantities can be precisely measured—like equal pay for equal work. But in marriage we are much more concerned with quality than with quantity, and equity expresses our goal much better.

Now let's apply all this to the resolution of conflict. Once we recognize that conflict is just disagreement heated up, and that disagreement arises out of differences that are accentuated when we try to live close together, we can see clearly that reconciling our differences is the main task in building a marriage. When people ask, "What do you mean by *working* on your marriage?" the answer we would give is, "It means reconciling our differences so that we can live harmoniously together." We often liken this to building a dry wall, fitting many stones together so that they match each other and create a firm, solid structure. In this sense, marriage can rightly be called an art. It takes time and effort to do this, and you'll never be completely finished—the pieces keep changing their shape so that they have to be refitted.

But when two people unite to reconcile the changes together, it can be a very pleasant and rewarding task.

Unfortunately, however, it isn't much use saying all this to the average married couple. Most of us don't take kindly to the idea of changing our behavior. The commonly accepted idea of marriage is that you find an attractive and talented person who will adorn and augment your own personality, while you stay exactly as you are. A moment's serious consideration will show how ridiculous it is to imagine that *both* of you can be doing this at the same time!

However, by adopting the concept of stability as the measure of a satisfactory marriage, our culture reinforces this idea, illogical as it is. Consequently, many people are annoyed, and even insulted, when it is suggested to them that they have to work at their marriage. Concepts like change and growth and potential disturb these people. It seems not to occur to them that real rewards in any field of human endeavor require making intelligent plans, learning special skills, and putting in hard effort. How high must our divorce rate go before we face the obvious?

Most couples, therefore, faced with conflict, get angry with each other and find themselves unable to negotiate. When they try to resolve a disagreement, they get into a fight, or they feel too hurt to go on communicating and pull back. You *can't* negotiate when you are angry. You can't see the issues straight; you can't accept the other person's view; you can't make concessions. So anger blocks the way to negotiation. Loving couples find their hopes shattered, their patience worn down. They end up disillusioned and disenchanted. It isn't that they have failed to negotiate their differences. They never get to the point at which they have a fair chance to negotiate at all; they are too angry and too hurt.

That's why resolving anger—defusing the bomb—is of central importance. But once the anger is out of the way, the process of negotiation can go right ahead. So let's look at that process.

At the heart of every conflict, as we have seen, there is

difference. You want one thing; I want another. We can illustrate this by a simple diagram (see diagram 3). We begin with the husband at one end of a line and the wife at the other. The line represents the difference that separates them. They want to be together, but they find themselves apart.

There are three ways of dealing with this situation. The task of negotiation is to find out which of the three alternatives offers the best possibility of reconciliation in a given situation. They all begin with the letter *C.*

The first possible solution is by *capitulation.* The husband says: "All right. I see how much you want a new washing machine. I'd prefer not to spend the money at this time. But I

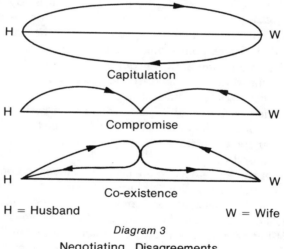

H = Husband   W = Wife

Diagram 3

Negotiating Disagreements

love you, and I want to make life as comfortable for you as I can, so I'll give in." Or the wife, in a different situation, may say: "You know it's awkward for me, and for the kids, to wait until six-thirty for dinner. But I have listened to your explanations, and I can see how hard it is for you to get home before six o'clock, and I

119

understand that you need time to unwind before eating. So, OK, we'll do this for your sake, as a token of our love."

Some people feel that capitulation is not negotiation but surrender. We don't agree. Our dictionary includes among the definitions of capitulation, "to acquiesce," "to come to terms"; and the word *capitulation* comes from the Latin meaning "to draw up under heads or chapters"—in other words—"to draft an agreement." The instances we have given show that capitulation need not be anything resembling a humiliating process; it can in fact be a loving gift.

There are, however, two important rules that should govern capitulation in negotiating marital disagreements. The first is that it should never be exacted by coercion—that is, by force or pressure—but should be freely offered. The second is that one partner should not habitually capitulate to the other; rather, over any period of time, both should take turns. An appropriate act of capitulation between a loving couple should leave both feeling good. If this doesn't happen, something has gone wrong, and the situation should be investigated.

Referring back to the diagram, capitulation is shown by the husband going all the way over to the wife's side to stand behind her, or by the wife going all the way over to the husband's side.

The second option is *compromise*. It means meeting in the middle or somewhere along the line, and it involves concessions made on both sides. This is the time-honored "horse trading" technique. The husband, for example, wants to go fishing on the couple's only upcoming free weekend, but the wife wants them to visit her parents. The two finally agree that they will drive to the wife's home on Friday evening and spend the evening with her parents. All day Saturday, the husband will go off fishing, and the wife will spend the afternoon with him by the lake. On Sunday morning, they will go to church with the in-laws, and on Sunday afternoon, they will drive home together. In this particular compromise, the husband thinks he has made rather more concessions than the wife; but she is pleased, and he knows he will get a chance to try the fishing in an unfamiliar lake. They both accept the plan, and it goes well. Next time, the wife will be in a mood to make the major concession.

Some people also dislike the word *compromise.* One of our dictionary definitions reads: "something midway between different things, or combining certain of their qualities." The illustration we have given shows how a couple can balance out the making of concessions so as to maintain equity in their relationship.

The compromise section of diagram 3 shows a situation in which husband and wife both go halfway and meet at a middle point. Their point of meeting could, in fact, be anywhere along the line that represents the difference between them.

The third option available in negotiation is *coexistence,* which means an agreement to accept the current difference, because at the present time it seems impossible for either to give ground to the other. The circling movements of husband and wife shown in diagram 3 are intended to show that each of them has made a sincere effort to move over to the side of the other, or to find a point between them at which they could both agree to settle. But this is not always possible, and we must not expect it to be. The partners in marriage are two distinct individuals in their own right, and there can be no true love between two people who do not respect and affirm each other's personhood. It may be inconvenient, and even painful, for you to recognize the fact that there are differences between you and your spouse that cannot at the moment be reconciled; but acceptance of this is much better for a relationship than either a pretended agreement that the difference doesn't really exist or, worse still, a capitulation of one to the other achieved by coercion.

Admittedly, this last solution is the hardest one to live with. But we ourselves have found that accepting coexistence has, over time, deepened our understanding of each other and even our respect for each other. We have found, also, that when two people truly love each other, and no pressure is exerted on either side, the gap between them often narrows and even closes as time passes.

Our experience of marriage counseling has shown us that coexistence is particularly difficult for couples who are deeply alienated from each other and therefore have no accumulated fund of mutual love or goodwill in their relationship. When people truly love each other, that love includes a deep confidence and trust, and this makes it relatively easy and natural to allow your partner a large measure of freedom to be different.

We have also found in counseling that some differences between the partners are much harder to live with than others. A few obvious examples come to mind—a couple pursuing different vocations that could be reconciled only by their working in widely separated communities, a marriage in which one considered extramarital sex acceptable and the other didn't, strong convictions on the part of both partners that the children should be raised under different and conflicting conditions, opposing standards of honesty and integrity. We have known marriages that have continued to be meaningful despite apparently clashing value systems, but we admit that this calls for a great deal of mutual tolerance.

However, at this point we reach the frontier beyond which we have to face the fact that a marriage may not be capable of functioning at all, and separation and divorce may be the only solution in the best interest of all concerned. This situation has to be faced when it occurs, but our impression is that a great many divorces today are not a result of irreconcilable differences, but rather of inability to make adjustments that could, with adequate insight and resources, be successfully achieved.

During experiences of successful negotiation, a marriage grows continually. This is what we mean by the creative use of conflict. Negotiation means the willingness to understand and the willingness to change. In settling differences by sharing what is in our minds, we disclose our inner selves more and more clearly to each other. By making concessions and adjusting ourselves to new patterns of behavior that enable our relationship to run smoothly, we explore and develop our potentials and learn to be flexible as we meet life's ever-changing demands. It is often said that being married is a restraining and confining influence on personal growth. Our experience has provided no confirmation for that view. Indeed, we have found the opposite to be true.

We hope you can now see clearly how our concept of the three essentials for a happy marriage has developed. All three are needed, and all must operate together. Without a commitment to growth, few couples will make the effort to learn how to work on their relationship. They will make a series of unsuccessful attempts, become discouraged, then give up and settle for mediocrity and superficiality. But even with a real commitment to growth, few couples can get very far without a clear understanding of what are really complex processes, or without the very helpful tools that are now available for facilitating that understanding.

You can see also how vitally important it is for a couple to learn to communicate. Without this skill, how can they hope to know and understand each other at the deep levels at which their feelings and intentions are functioning? Without this knowledge, the best they can do is simply guess at each other's real needs and live with each other groping in semidarkness.

Yet communication, however important, is not in itself enough. Even when a couple are aware of each other's functioning, action is needed to deal with the differences and disagreements that inevitably arise between them. This requires the motivation that comes from commitment. It also requires the ability to find an acceptable way of resolving anger, so that two committed people can move through their conflicts to the kinds of resolution that will progressively strengthen and deepen the unity and harmony of their relationship.

That's a lot to ask of any couple. But don't forget that we offer an awful lot in return—the reward of a truly happy marriage.

17
Work Units for Fifth and Sixth Weeks

The goal for these final units should be quite clear. It is to enable you to experiment with the ideas we have just presented—making use of conflict to promote growth in your relationship, resolving anger together, and learning to negotiate disagreements effectively.

Since the six-week period ends on a Friday, we suggest that you consider spending an extra two-hour period on the following Saturday in order to evaluate the whole program and make an ongoing growth plan. Although this is not part of your contract, we will include some directions for it in the hope that you will consider rounding out the program in this way.

Schedule for Fifth Week

Preparation: Read or reread chapters 14, 15, and 16.

Saturday: Two-hour session
First hour (H leads)—Exercise on anger
Second hour (W leads)—Positive interaction exercise

Sunday to
Friday: Twenty minutes daily—Sharing time (H and W lead alternate days.)

Directions

The first hour of your two-hour session this week will be used to look at your anger patterns. In this exercise, you should take fifteen minutes first to write notes in response to the following:

1. Recall three to five recent situations in which you experienced anger. Include if possible some in which the anger was directed against your marriage partner.

2. What is your characteristic anger pattern? What stages do you normally go through, from first awareness of your anger until it is finally cleared up?

3. What progress have you made, as a couple, in accepting each other's anger and in helping each other to resolve the anger? Do you see it as important for your marriage that this type of harmony should be achieved?

After you have completed the exercise, discuss your reflections together, and consider how you can learn to deal effectively with anger as it develops in your relationship.

By way of contrast, your second exercise will be one we call positive interaction, although it might as easily be named mutual affirmation. It really comes under the heading of "Couple Communication," but we decided to introduce it at this point so that you could look at your negative and your positive feelings together—one after the other—in the same session.

We want to make the point that in a relationship, negative and positive feelings are related to each other. The opposite of love isn't really hate; it is cold indifference. When people are fighting each other, they are at least interacting. They are involved with each other, and given a relationship of any kind, there is always the possibility that negative hostility can be turned into positive regard. Moreover, a refusal on the part of a married couple to face their negative feelings and to bring them out into the open always has the effect of blocking off the potential flow of positive feelings between them. That's why couples who suppress their anger against each other cannot be genuinely tender and affectionate. Although we personally don't encourage venting anger in a love relationship, because we think there is a much better way of dealing with it, we nevertheless recognize that couples who fight (with reasonable restraint) can be tender and affectionate in the intervals between one fight and the next! They can also, however, be even more tender and affectionate without fighting at all!

So here's the positive interaction exercise. We suggest that you sit facing each other and hold hands if you are comfortable in doing so. The exercise is very simple—you tell each other some of the things about each other that you really appreciate. We would like you, however, to do it in a special way. We have done this ourselves very often, and we find this way to be best.

Instead of a back-and-forth dialogue, decide who will go first, and take only one turn each. Look into each other's eyes while you talk, and address each other directly by name. Do the exercise in a reflective, unhurried way, with pauses whenever you like. During your turn, think of a number of qualities in your partner, and share them slowly one by one, beginning each with: "I love you because . . ."; or "I like you when . . ."; or "Another thing I especially like about you is . . ."; or similar words that come naturally to you.

We find that most couples have never done this before—not even in their courting days. This is a great pity, but it's never too late to start! You may find it a little embarrassing at first—that's the "taboo on tenderness" holding you back. Some husbands particularly find it difficult to get started because of the "stiff upper lip" philosophy men are supposed to observe. But let us assure you—this is the one place that that philosophy doesn't apply. So go right ahead and defy the taboo. If your voice quavers with emotion, just let it quaver. If tears should come into your eyes, let them come. Warm positive emotion between husband and wife is the healthiest kind of emotion we know.

Take plenty of time with the exercise, and talk about it afterwards—how you felt, how you reacted to what was said to you. Furthermore, once you have gone through this experience, do it again from time to time—not often enough to make it routine, but as something to be reserved for special occasions.

The plan for your daily sessions, this week and the next, is called *sharing time*. Something new? No, just our old friend the daily dialogue, but in a rather different form. Instead of the first ten minutes of the separate writing-down of your reflections, then exchanging notebooks and discussions, we suggest that you try using the whole twenty minutes together. At first, take a few minutes to make brief individual notes of things to be shared; then talk about them together. On a later occasion, try doing it without making notes at all—just a few minutes of silent reflection together—and then share whatever thoughts come to you.

Let us explain what lies behind this. Our hope is that you will, for the rest of your married life, take time for daily dialogue together. Nothing you could now decide to do could have a more far-reaching influence on your life together. A study was once made to find out how much time average married couples spend together talking directly about their relationship. The study came up with an average period of twenty-three minutes a week! How can a loving relationship possibly be nurtured on such a starvation diet? If you want to know why so many American marriages are in trouble, you need look no further than this for an explanation.

With this in mind, we hope you will make a commitment to each other to honor the daily sharing time. But feel free to carry it out in whatever way (or at whatever time) suits you best—don't follow some rigid formula. We know one couple who set the alarm clock to wake them early so they can talk in the morning—before getting out of bed. One husband we know insists on coming home daily for a quiet lunch (and sharing hour) with his wife. Others prefer to do their sharing the last thing at night. The details don't matter. What does matter is making it a daily discipline. And we strongly recommend your beginning by sharing feelings, then sharing thoughts about your relationship, then anything else you like.

For people for whom personal religion is important, this can include Bible reading, prayer, or other religious activities. We have deliberately not introduced religious practices into this book, because we know that they differ very widely from one couple to another, and we don't want couples who are not religious to feel that anything is being imposed upon them. For us, as Quakers, our sharing times have a very close association with our religious faith.

Schedule for Sixth Week

Preparation:	Reread chapters 14, 15, and 16.
Saturday:	Two-hour session First hour (W leads)—Exercise on negotiation Second hour (H leads)—Growth plan and contracts
Sunday to Friday:	Twenty minutes daily—Sharing time (H and W lead alternate days.)
Saturday:	Optional two-hour session for final evaluation

Directions

For the exercise on negotiation, take fifteen minutes to write down your responses to the following:

1. List all issues you know of that are now under negotiation between you and your partner, or that ought to be.
2. How do you personally react to the bargaining process in marriage? Do you have any difficulties with it?

3. How do you feel your partner reacts to the process of negotiation? Does this create any difficulties for you?

Spend the rest of the hour sharing your reflections, discussing them, and trying to reach agreement on some specific issues.

The next hour should be spent preparing a growth plan for your marriage. You did this experimentally before, and you might look again at that early plan. You should, however, have learned a lot since then, and you should be ready to develop it a good deal in consequence.

Here's a simple exercise to help you get started. Each of you should take ten minutes to write down, separately, short lists under the following three headings: (1) what I want for *me*, (2) what I want for *you,* (3) what I want for *us.* Then share what you have written separately, and you're ready to put your growth plan together.

This plan can be for the next month, the next six months, the next year—whatever you both think would be best for you. The time should be specified, however, and each item should be open for renegotiation. We won't give you detailed instructions for making the plan—except to say that it should be a statement of intention, put down in writing, signed by both of you, and kept for future reference. It should indicate in what areas you agree to work on your marriage during the specified time.

You may want to build contracts into your growth plan. If so, they also should be put in writing. A contract is just a very specific agreement arrived at between the two of you, spelling out clearly what each of you undertakes to do.

We want to sound a word of warning here. Contracts can be very useful. They provide evidence of your commitment to each other. However, *all contracts should be renegotiable.* If either of you, or both of you, should fail to do what you agreed to do, the contract should at once be canceled or revised. It is bad for your morale to have written and signed agreements around that are not being carried out.

The best plan is to make contracts for only short periods of time and for limited undertakings that will be quite easy to carry out. It's far better to agree to take one simple step, and really to take it, than to promise the world and fail to follow through. What we say to couples is, "If you can only jump over a three-foot wall, but you keep trying to jump over a four-foot wall, you are only going to hurt yourself." So contract to do something quite simple, something you really mean to carry out; and *do* carry it out. Then, contract for the next step.

For your daily dialogue this week, continue the sharing time in whatever way suits you best. This will bring you to the end of your six-week program with us. We have suggested, however, that you take a final two-hour period to make a final evaluation. This is optional, but we'd like you to do it if you are willing.

The evaluation should be an attempt to sum up together what this total experience over the past six weeks has meant to you. If you care to, make a copy of the evaluation form in Appendix E, fill it out, and mail it to us. We won't send you a personal reply, but we assure you that we will certainly *read* what you send to us. We ask for your response because it is through the evaluations we get from couples who share our programs that we are constantly developing new and better ideas.

PART V
Where Do We Go from Here?

18
Looking Back and Looking Forward

We promised you a lot when you undertook to work with us for this six-week period, didn't we? Yet if you as a couple have faithfully carried out the program we planned for you, here are some of the rewards you should have already reaped.

1. *You should have a clearer picture of where your marriage now is.* You should know what progress you have already made, and you will, we hope, be thankful for that. There must be very few husbands and wives, however severe their present troubles, who can't look back without finding a good deal to be thankful for. The old practice of counting your blessings is still a very worthwhile activity, though somewhat neglected in these days.

2. *You should have a pretty good idea of what you still want to achieve in your marriage.* You should have identified areas in which you look for improvement, including the gains you hope to make and the potential you plan to appropriate. Your future expectations should not be wild and impossible dreams but realistic and attainable goals that you can reasonably hope to achieve.

3. *You should have developed some new skills* that you can use in the process of getting from where you are now to where

you hope to be. You should be able to communicate better, to share your feelings and needs more deeply and more openly with each other. You should have a more positive and constructive approach to the conflicts that arise between you and know how to free them from destructive anger and resolve them creatively by the process of negotiation.

4. As a result of these gains, *you should be feeling happier about your relationship.* You should enjoy the sense of fulfillment that comes from making new beginnings in the direction of creative growth and change. There should be a deeper sense of companionship between the two of you because you know each other better as persons. Above all, there should be a warm flow of new affection, tenderness, and love that gives you a sense of gratitude for each other and, individually, a new sense of worth.

Does this seem a lot to expect for twenty-four hours of following our instructions over a period of six weeks? We don't think so. One of the exciting things we have found in working with couples is that positive changes in attitudes can take place quite quickly when the partners really act, sincerely and wholeheartedly, together. We are not saying that lasting changes in behavior don't require a lot of time and effort. But a change in *attitude* can come, as a great source of encouragement and motivation, as soon as a couple make a solemn commitment to growth, and particularly when, by taking a few courageous steps, they prove to themselves that they *do* have the power to make real progress. The great thing is to break out of the prison of long-established habits (and the pessimistic outlook that they tend to create) and to start walking together in a new direction. This can be as dramatic as a religious conversion. In fact, in some ways it *is* a religious conversion. It is a rebirth within us of faith in the capacities with which we have been endowed and of the conviction that our dreams were given us, not to mock us, but to be translated into reality.

We want to offer you some further guidance about the tasks that still lie ahead. But first, we would like to pause for a moment to say something to any couples who have not traveled thus far with us. Let's try to see why this might have happened.

1. *You never really got started on the program.* Maybe you felt cynical about the whole idea, or you didn't believe the claims we made. You continued to read but remained unconvinced. Obviously, we can't expect everyone to agree with us, but we thank you for at least giving us a hearing.

But perhaps you couldn't start because only one partner was willing, and it is obvious that it takes two, working together, to carry out the program. We're sorry if you two couldn't manage to agree, at this time, to take the plunge. We can only renew our invitation to you (if at some later time the "dragee" should come to see the situation in a different light) to join us when the right time comes.

2. *You started, but you didn't keep it up.* We wonder why. It could be that some unexpected event—a change in your life situation, a crisis in your relationship—upset your plans. In that event, you may be able to start again at a later time. It is possible that you didn't find the exercises entirely suited to your needs. Obviously, it is hard to meet the requirements of all kinds of couples, at all different stages in their relationship, with one simple formula. Yet we have tried hard to do just that; and if we have failed in your case, we'd be glad to have your suggestions for improvement.

Another possibility is that you found the program challenging you to take steps you were not willing to take, and you backed down and gave up. We are saddened when this happens, but we do know, from our own experience, that a price has to be paid for the better quality of relationship we want for you. There's no way in which we can reduce that price, because every worthwhile achievement in life has to be paid for in accordance with its value. We can only hope that you two may one day decide to give it another try.

3. *You completed the entire program, but your relationship is no better.* This really troubles us, and we'd like to hear from you. As we have already said, we are so confident about the value and effectiveness of what we have to offer that we are almost ready to guarantee results. We can only wonder in your case whether you understood the directions clearly or whether you both are really committed to the program in spirit as well as in action. Were there, in either of you, hidden reservations? If not, and you still want to work effectively on your marriage, we can only conclude that in your special circumstances you may need the interpretation and support that a counselor could provide. We suggest you read what we will have to say later about seeking counseling help.

Now let's come back to the couples who have successfully completed the program. We want, before we finish, to offer you some further guidance as well as some resources you can use in continuing to seek marital growth—a process, we would remind you again, that never ends.

You may wonder why we have said very little about specific areas of the marriage relationship that get a lot of attention in most books written for the guidance of couples—including books we ourselves have written in earlier years. For example, in the marriage potential test, we asked you to score yourselves in areas like gender roles, sexual fulfillment, money management, parent effectiveness, and decision-making; yet we have subsequently made very little reference to any of these. Why not?

That's a fair question. We are fully aware that we have seemed to ignore what are often regarded as the major issues in marriage. And we have done this quite deliberately, because we are becoming increasingly convinced they are *not* the major issues. We have devoted long years to counseling with couples about these issues, and we have evidence that we were able to help these couples. But we have begun to see the whole matter in a rather different perspective.

In the past, most programs designed to help couples have been conducted in the manner of problem-solving. As we have already indicated, we are increasingly uncomfortable about using the word *problem* with respect to marriage because it has come to mean something like what happens when a car or refrigerator fails to function and has to be repaired by a mechanic. We think this plays into the false view that sees a good marriage as a *stable* marriage. Frankly, we don't think stable marriages *are* necessarily good marriages. They are often dreary, dull, and only half-alive. So the idea of repairing a marriage would suggest restoring it to its previous state of stability. What we want to do is to bring the marriage to life and get it growing. We therefore prefer to talk about "obstacles" to growth that confront the couple as they move forward together.

Instead of "repairers" of marriage, we think marriage counselors should progressively become "trainers" and "consultants" to couples, helping them to draw on their own skills and resources in order to develop their own potentials.

When we take this approach, we see clearly that what is important is to equip as many couples as possible with the skills and tools necessary to develop their own relationships. And we are now quite convinced that this means helping them to focus on what we see as the "three essentials": commitment to growth, an effective communication system, and the creative use of conflict (see chap. 4). Armed with these skills and tools, they should have a reasonable chance of overcoming most obstacles they are likely to encounter.

It isn't that we think that all couples can succeed without help. But we think that trying to help them to overcome particular obstacles, without first helping them to marshal their own resources, is putting the cart before the horse. Achieving the three essentials is, in our opinion, the primary task for any married couple to fulfill. Making adjustments in the other areas of marriage is secondary, in that these areas are not, as is often believed, the *causes* of marital failure. They are, rather, the particular areas of interaction in which the failure of a marriage to function is both inwardly revealed and outwardly displayed.

In the next chapter, we will try to illustrate this by going over some of these secondary areas and offering guidance to couples who may need help in dealing with them.

In the final chapters of the book, we shall offer some further resources for your use in continuing to pursue marital growth beyond the basic beginnings you have already made.

19
Some Secondary Areas of Marital Adjustment

Marriage is a complex relationship that involves two people in adjusting to each other in a great many areas of living. Writers and researchers have listed as many as forty such areas in which difficulties could occur, and these forty could be further divided up or added to.

In this chapter, we'll select a few representative areas and try to illustrate what we have already explained—that these are in our opinion secondary areas for adjustment and can normally be handled successfully by couples who have already acquired the three essentials. We sometimes call these three essentials a "primary coping system."

We will pick up the areas, additional to the three essentials, that are listed in the marriage potential test. Here they are.

1. *Common Goals and Values.* Involved here would be your religious beliefs, your ethical standards, and the causes you support and work for. Obviously, it is helpful if you begin marriage by being close together in the positions you take on these matters. When there are wide differences, a marriage can be put under considerable strain, because the ways in which we behave are usually the practical outcome of our goals and

139

values. If, however, you can both communicate clearly and honestly what your values are, this should help you very much to get into constructive and ongoing dialogue that will lead to mutual understanding and respect. If disagreements arise between you because of your differences, you can use the processes of negotiation to find workable solutions. If the going gets rough, your commitment to growth should give you the necessary perseverance to go on working and to make progress.

2. *Appreciation and Affection.* We have pointed out that the supreme quality found in strong families is that they constantly affirm each other. Couples who fail to do this usually have difficulty expressing positive feelings, a quite common obstacle in our culture. Realizing the importance of showing appreciation and affection (and getting over your shyness about declaring your love) should open the way for you to give your partner more and more encouragement and praise. We have already given you a start in this direction through the exercise on positive interaction you have done as part of the program. And we have emphasized again and again the importance of sharing your feelings—especially your positive feelings.

3. *Agreement on Gender Roles.* The important word here is of course *agreement*. There are still couples who hold tenaciously to the belief that the husband should have the final word in all decisions and that the wife can best contribute to the marriage by playing a subservient role. So long as *both* of you accept this view, you are not likely to run into trouble. Indeed in a one-vote system, a great deal of conflict can be avoided. On the other hand, there are couples who are committed to a marriage with no fixed roles, in which all functions in the marriage (except childbearing!) are fully interchangeable. Operating this kind of system isn't easy, because it is so completely new; but couples committed to it are usually pioneers and are therefore highly motivated to prove that the system will work.

The couples who have the real trouble fall into two categories.

First, there are those who are in transition from the old system to the new. This can be rough going. But open communication (and willingness to suffer the inconvenience and pain that often go with change) should give such couples the resources they need. In addition, it can be especially helpful for them to get into a couples' growth group where they can learn from, and get support from, other couples who are working through the same adjustments. We shall be describing how couples' groups function in a later chapter.

Most difficult of all is the plight of those who are deeply divided about the issue of gender roles. The most usual situation is the one in which the husband expects the wife to accept the traditional subordinate role, while she insists on the freedom and autonomy that, as emphasized by the women's liberation movement, are her rights. The resulting crisis, if there is no willingness to compromise on either side, may be one of the most frequent causes of broken marriage in our society today. We have already discussed this in chapter 7.

4. *Cooperation and Teamwork.* This concerns all the things you do together inside and outside the home and the extent to which you support and encourage each other in private and in public. A loving couple will naturally be sensitive and considerate toward each other; they will be ready to offer help when it is needed.

This area of marriage, however, has become greatly complicated today by the changes in the concepts of gender roles we have discussed above. Where the traditional view is held, and the wife's duties are mainly confined to homemaking, a fairly clear division of functions has already been established. The situation in which the wife works outside the home is, however, much more complicated, because the husband finds that he is expected to undertake a major share of the household chores, and this may be completely contrary to his expectations of marriage. Working out a good distribution of responsibilities under these conditions can be quite difficult. This area of

141

marriage and marriage enrichment is very well treated in Charlotte Clinebell's *Meet Me in the Middle* (see Appendix B).

5. *Sexual Fulfillment.* This area of marriage has been getting an enormous amount of attention in recent years. Great advances have been made in correcting the negative, repressive attitudes of the past. One of the interesting developments has been the shift from preoccupation with anatomy and physiology, and with the learning of techniques, to the more enlightened emphasis of Masters and Johnson, who have made it clear that striving for sexual performance as such is self-defeating. The new sex therapy sees good sexual functioning as depending on *the quality of the total relationship* between husband and wife, and it puts the emphasis on working with the "marital unit," often with the aid of co-therapists, one of each sex. There is great stress also on open communication about feelings and needs and on learning by trying out new approaches. The emphasis on "sensate focus" encourages the couple to touch and caress each other in ways that come naturally and spontaneously to all couples who are truly and warmly in love with each other.

We would say that doing the exercises we have given you in this book should, directly or indirectly, open up the way for the improvement of your sex relationship. Masters and Johnson have repeatedly emphasized that sexual functioning is a *natural* process and cannot be contrived. Loving partners who can communicate effectively will almost certainly find ways and means of meeting each other's sexual needs, just as they help each other to meet their needs in other areas. If, however, having enriched your marriage in other ways, you are still falling short on sexual fulfillment, we would encourage you to seek the help of a competent sex therapist. We must stress the word *competent* because unfortunately there are many quacks in this field at the present time. One way to locate a reliable therapist is to find one who is certified by the American Association of Sex Educators, Counselors, and Therapists—AASECT (5010 Wisconsin Avenue, NW, Suite 304, Washington, D.C. 20016)—

which is so far the only organization that grants certification, on a national basis, in this new field.

6. *Money Management.* The American system of "Do it now—pay later" makes financial trouble a frequently occurring difficulty in many marriages. A great many young people today are not adequately prepared when it comes to budgeting, handling a checkbook, or understanding interest charges. We need to provide more adequate services to married couples in the field of financial counseling.

We have found again and again in our marriage counseling, however, that mismanaging money can also be the result of emotional insecurity. Americans are encouraged to believe that owning things is the gateway to happiness, and that houses, cars, clothes, are not just useful resources for living but are also status symbols. So an unhappy wife will go on a spending spree in order to bolster her faltering self-esteem, and a husband with a low self-image will spend foolishly to make an impression on friends and colleagues. A couple in conflict will find in their money management (or mismanagement) a readily available battlefield on which to fight out their unresolved differences and disagreements.

One wife with whom we worked gave herself zero on money management in the marriage potential test. Her explanation was that before marriage she had managed her money well, but in attempts at joint management with her husband, she just couldn't function at all. Obviously, the financial deadlock was simply the reflection of a deeper interpersonal conflict that they had been unable to resolve.

On the other hand, if self-esteem and emotional security are sustained by the warmth and mutual appreciation that a loving relationship creates, then money management simply becomes a matter of common sense. Most of us have enough of the latter to enable us to manage our money, but it goes out of the window when sinking self-esteem takes over and drives us compulsively to spend what we haven't got and to buy what we can't afford.

143

7. *Parent Effectiveness.* You may have wondered why in a book of this kind we have up to now made no direct reference to parenthood, which is such an obviously important part of many marriages. Failure to refer to this has again been deliberate on our part. Why?

Over and over, we have noticed that both individual couples and society in general tend to evade the subject of marriage, and to deflect discussions about family life to other aspects, such as homes, incomes, social rehabilitation, and—especially—children. We don't say these issues are not important. What we *do* say, though, is that in facing the current crisis in family life, we must put first things first. And the first clear, obvious fact to be faced is that you can't build a great family on the foundation of a poor marriage.

It therefore seems obvious to us that if all the marriages in the world could somehow be enabled to realize something like their full potential, most of our family problems—and most of our other social problems too, for that matter—would simply go away. The fact that we stubbornly refuse to see this, and to act on it, is the best evidence we can find that human beings, for all their intelligence and high standards of education, have not yet learned to act rationally when their own best interests are involved. You have absolutely nothing to lose, and a very great deal to gain, in working for a loving, harmonious marriage, instead of a miserable, conflict-ridden one.

The same may be said for your children. The greatest contribution you can make to their welfare is to provide them with the priceless gift of a loving, happy home. In such a setting, children feel warmly secure. This produces exactly the environment they need for healthy emotional development. Beyond all other things you can do for your children, nothing matters more than giving them the kind of parental love that flows from a father and mother who love each other dearly.

All that you are learning about improving your marriage can also be applied to your relationship with your children. We have often been told by couples who have started working seriously on their relationship to each other that one of the first results of their efforts is a dramatic change in their relationship to their children. The things you are learning about communication, about dealing with anger, about resolving conflicts, all apply directly also to parent-child relationships. As soon as you begin to get your marriage functioning at higher levels, you can start working in the same way with your children. And if you want it all spelled out in specific terms, read Thomas Gordon's book *Parent Effectiveness Training*. Better still, find out where in your neighborhood you can sign up together to take the P.E.T. course.

8. *Decision-making.* This is an easy one. The making of decisions together is simply an effective combination of good communication, which gets all your options out in the open, and the effective use of negotiation, which brings you as near to agreement as you can hope for. That's really all there is to it.

We have used these eight areas of adjustment in marriage to demonstrate that once you have the three essentials, you should be well equipped to deal with most of the secondary difficulties that are likely to crop up in your relationship. You can test this out, if you like, in other areas. Here are a few: recreation, religion, relating to friends and relatives, career choices, political action, community involvement. You yourselves can think of others to add to the list. In a growing marriage, there is no end to the adjustments and readjustments that need to be made as you move through life's successive phases. To be unable to cope with these endless adjustments, because you are committed to stability in your marriage, can be a constant source of frustration and misery. On the other hand, to have a flexible, growing marriage, and to be ready to make changes and use new experiences creatively, keeps life exciting and purposeful.

20
Working with a Marriage Counselor

Let us make one point very clear. Nothing in this book should be construed as implying that well-qualified marriage counselors are not needed to make a necessary and important contribution to the promotion of happy marriages.

Occasionally, people who have heard us talk about marriage enrichment gain the impression that we are suggesting that with the development of these new positive and preventive approaches, counseling with married couples has become outdated and redundant.

This is certainly *not* our view. The record will show that we have devoted a major part of our professional lives to the promotion of marriage counseling services all over the world. We do not regret having devoted so much time to this. We have seen marriage counseling pass through early, experimental stages, improve its procedures, and become more and more effective. The really competent marriage counselor of today is a very valuable member of the professional community. Investigation and research have established beyond all doubt that given a reasonable chance, a qualified marriage counselor can do a great deal for a couple confronted with difficulties they are unable to resolve by their own unaided efforts. We only wish that more couples in trouble would seek counseling—and particularly that they would seek it earlier than they usually do.

We have come to feel, however, that marriage counseling alone, as we understand it today, cannot provide the whole answer. The counselor's emphasis, as it is widely understood, is remedial. Counseling is frequently seen as a rescue operation. This is effectively illustrated by the title of the well-known series of magazine articles entitled "Can This Marriage Be Saved?" We have become firmly convinced that marriage counselors far too often get into the act too late to be able to provide the most effective service that could be rendered. There will always be a need for remedial service, because there will always be couples who fail to face the tensions building up in their marriage until an explosion occurs. But obviously, what we need to do is not to stand by and let marriages sink deeper and deeper into trouble, then rush in with the ambulance, but to train couples in the use of techniques that will *keep them out of trouble*—a practice we now know to be entirely possible in many cases.

A text in the Bible sums it all up very neatly: "These ought ye to have done, and not to leave the other undone."

There is much evidence, which gratifies us greatly, that marriage counseling *is* beginning to make this shift. In fact, most marriage counselors would much rather work with couples preventively, because they would see a much greater return for their efforts that way. The difficulty is in fact not with the marriage counselor, but in the unwilling attitude toward getting help about marriage that exists in our culture, arising out of the static concept of marriage we still hold so tenaciously.

Clark Vincent, an esteemed professional colleague of ours, has called this the "myth of naturalism"—the widespread idea that marriage is not an undertaking that requires any special knowledge or skill. The view is that getting married is like a duckling going into water for the first time; all the equipment needed to swim successfully is built in, and it goes into operation immediately and automatically. Of course, this is manifestly untrue of marriage, as our high rates of divorce make abundantly clear. But in spite of all evidence to the contrary, this is still the basis of our cultural attitudes.

Consequently, anyone who thinks he has to "learn" about marriage, or to seek help in order to make a marriage work, is regarded as a deficient and incompetent person and looked down upon. When couples feel the need for help, therefore, they are very reluctant to admit it, even to their best friends. When you have a toothache or a stomachache that won't go away, you make an appointment to see the dentist or the doctor, and you don't feel any need to do this under a cloak of great secrecy. But if you get a marriage ache, you feel ashamed and guilty, and you conceal it as long as you possibly can. Only when the pain is unendurable do you brace yourself to seek the aid of a counselor; and by that time, it may be too late.

This foolish attitude has got to change, and it will change. But meanwhile, a marriage counselor who decides to concentrate on helping couples at the preventive level simply can't make a living. As long as pathology pays and prevention doesn't, most marriage counselors will have no choice but to spend most of their time dealing with pathology.

We have a somewhat similar situation, of course, in the field of medicine. Dr. John Knowles, a physician who is now president of the Rockefeller Foundation, contributed to *Time* magazine (August 1, 1976) a brilliant essay on the health needs of the American people. He indicated that nearly all the major diseases that plagued people in the past are now largely under control, or are soon likely to be. He then went on to say that "the next major advances in the health of the American people will result from the assumption of individual responsibility for one's own health," and added that we now know most of what we need to know in order to live a long and healthy life. The real task of medicine today is therefore to communicate this knowledge widely to all citizens and to persuade them to benefit from it.

The same may be said for marriage. In our opinion, it is not at all necessary for families to be breaking up at the present disturbing rate. Most of them could be functioning successfully if they followed the relatively simple rules we have laid down in this book. As yet, however, these rules are not widely known. The public understanding of marriage is sadly deficient.

Of course, even if the rules for achieving a happy marriage were more widely understood, there would be some people who would ignore them, just as there are some people who ignore the rules of good health and have to take the resulting pathology to the physician. It is our conviction, however, that these people are in the minority. The vast majority of people in this country could be convinced that it would pay them handsomely to follow the guidelines for successful marriage.

By working to bring about a change in their public image, we believe that marriage counselors could become a powerful force in getting this done. It is our hope that they will accept this challenge. We are quite optimistic about it.

Consequently, we want you to be aware of the resources a marriage counselor can offer you. He (or she) could help you to work through the program we have outlined in this book. We are well aware that some couples will lack the sustained motivation to carry out the program alone. But to work on it at home and make regular reports to your marriage counselor, enjoying the great benefit of his encouragement, his support, and his interpretation of procedures that aren't clear to you, could make all the difference. The material in this book will be quite familiar to any counselor who has kept up with recent developments in his field.

In addition, a counselor can give you the help you need in dealing with particular difficulties that get in your way—such personal troubles as excessive anxiety, depression, and hostility, and relational difficulties in areas like jealousy, sex, and gender roles. Any counselor would be delighted by a couple who have already made a serious commitment to work on their marriage and have already made some progress in the primary areas of communication and conflict resolution. The counselor's major difficulty is that so many of the couples who use his services just aren't motivated to do the work that is necessary in order to get the results they desire.

How do you go about finding the right counselor? Some guidance is necessary here.

In a few states—California, Georgia, Michigan, New Jersey, and Utah are examples—marriage counselors must be certified or licensed, so you wouldn't be likely to fall into the hands of outright quacks. Another useful safeguard would be to pick a clinical member of the American Association of Marriage and Family Counselors (AAMFC), which demands high standards of training and conformity to its Code of Ethics. We know this organization very well indeed, because we were its executive directors for seven years. You can check whether a counselor you have in mind is in the Directory of Clinical Members, if you have a copy available, or through the national headquarters office, which is located at 225 Yale Avenue, Claremont, California 91711.

Counselors who don't meet these requirements may nevertheless be quite competent, but you would have to investigate them on your own. Unfortunately, a professional qualification isn't of itself necessarily a reliable safeguard. Plenty of pastors, psychologists, psychiatrists, social workers, and guidance counselors have received no specific training whatsoever in marriage counseling as such; and some of them do quite poor work in this field. You should distrust, for example, a clinician who doesn't plan to work with you together as a couple (at least for some of the interviews), unless of course what you are seeking is individual treatment. On the other hand, a family therapist who wants to include your children in the counseling process would be all right, because he would fully understand the *relational* emphasis that is central to modern marriage counseling.

You can get some help by checking on a counselor's reputation with other local professionals—physicians, pastors, and lawyers who have referred couples to him or her. A competent counselor won't mind at all putting you in touch with such people. Also, marriage counselors working with recognized community agencies, such as a member agency of the Family Service Association of America, a university department of psychology or sociology, or a fully approved mental-health clinic, are likely to be well qualified or able to refer you if necessary to someone who is.

Don't commit yourself to a series of counseling interviews until you have had one session with the counselor and feel entirely happy about the way he has conducted the session. If during that session you develop real misgivings, it may be best not to continue. Successful counseling depends very much on what we call rapport—mutual confidence and trust between counselor and client—and it is doubtful whether this is likely to develop if you feel uncomfortable and strained during the first interview. If you decide not to go back, however, call and cancel the appointment. Don't be a "no show."

Although we have had to sound a few warnings, we would want finally to emphasize that most marriage counselors are well-trained, highly responsible, caring people, who are dedicated to their chosen profession. It is, however, unfortunate that there are a few who lack these qualities, and we would hate you to fall into the clutches of one of them. If you decide to use the services of a marriage counselor, we earnestly hope that you will find one in whom you can develop complete confidence. Good marriage counselors today, in comparison with what there was to offer in the past, are very good indeed. Happily, this is a field in which tremendous progress has been made.

151

21
Joining a Couples' Growth Group

One of the most powerful incentives for getting something done is arranging for a number of people to do it together. Most of us are not very good at taking the initiative alone. It's so easy to put projects off repeatedly and never get started; and it's so easy, having started, to get a little discouraged, or distracted, and give up. If others are involved with us, however, powerful new forces are set to work. Our self-esteem is likely to suffer if we fail to follow through. We are encouraged and inspired by the examples of others. We can reach out for support and help if we need it. United with others who are seeking the same goals, we can find new courage and confidence, new resolution and hope.

Well, why shouldn't couples work together on their marital growth? We don't yet know all we need to know about couples' groups, but as we accumulate knowledge and experience, we become more and more impressed by the possibilities. It may be well to remember that because of what we call the intermarital taboo, working with couples in groups is a procedure of quite recent origin. In the early days of marriage counseling, it was even considered inappropriate to work with husband and wife together. The rule in psychotherapy was one-to-one, and this thinking dominated the counseling field at that time. Therefore, if bringing even one couple together was regarded with suspicion, obviously bringing *several* couples together was almost unthinkable. A few pioneers dared to challenge this taboo, but group therapy for couples has developed slowly. Our own first experience of using it was in 1959.

By 1962, however, we were ready to venture to bring together, for a whole weekend, a group of couples who were *not* seeking counseling. They had what we tend to call normal marriages, but they were willing to look together at the possibilities of improving their relationships. We have continued to work with couples in groups ever since, and by now the fears about the dreadful things that might happen when several couples sat round in a circle and shared their experiences of marriage have been completely discredited.

By contrast, the history of growth groups for individuals has not gone anywhere near as smoothly. These groups have been described by various names—training labs, sensitivity training groups, encounter groups. There is solid evidence that many individuals who have taken part in these group experiences have found them very helpful; but unfortunately, there is also evidence that other individuals, far from being helped, were seriously harmed. This situation has been very carefully investigated, and it seems clear that the "casualties" resulted almost entirely either from poor leadership or from the use of what we call confrontation tactics. Unfortunately, however, the news about the casualties has spread widely, and the impression has been conveyed that if you get into one of these group experiences, it could turn out to be quite unpleasant.

We want to emphasize very strongly that none of this is true of couples' groups. We have been deeply involved in the marriage enrichment movement from its very beginning, and we have made careful inquiries among all the national agencies that sponsor such programs. Up to now, we have not been able to find any record of casualties of any kind. We believe this is due to the great care that has been taken by all the organizations concerned (most of them have some kind of religious affiliation) to forbid the use of confrontation in any form that could possibly make anyone feel threatened.

We are, therefore, beginning to develop with confidence all the promising possibilities that couples' groups offer for mutual growth and enrichment. This is taking place on an increasing scale across the country. If we include the Marriage Encounter program (which organizes couples' weekends, but involves couple interaction only to a very limited extent), it has been estimated that by now nearly one million couples have already undergone enrichment experiences in groups. And the evidence (including findings from several Ph.D. dissertations) supports our conviction that most of the couples have been greatly helped, while there is no solid evidence that any of them have suffered significant harm. All in all, this represents a remarkable record.

We would, therefore, give you every encouragement to take part in one of these group experiences if an opportunity should arise. We will tell you later how you can find out about these programs.

If you did take part in such a group, what would happen to you would resemble quite closely the program you have followed in this book. In fact, all the exercises and assignments we have given you have actually been developed and tested by couples in marriage enrichment groups that we have led.

Groups for marriage enrichment normally meet either continuously over a weekend or for one evening a week for a succession of six to eight weeks or more. The weekend meetings are often called couples' retreats (because couples participate in residence at a conference center or other suitable facility), while the weekly evening sessions are called couples' growth groups. Programs can vary, but broadly speaking there are three types of retreats. The Marriage Encounter, which exists in both the National and Worldwide versions, provides leadership in the form of a team of several experienced couples and a priest (or his equivalent in the Jewish and Protestant expressions). The team presents challenging talks, after which husbands and wives separate to write down their reflections in their notebooks; each couple then go off to their room to share these reflections in private dialogue. The program doesn't include any sharing of marital experiences between individual couples.

The second form is well represented by the Marriage Communication Labs started by The United Methodist Church. Now, a number of other religious groups have adopted the form. It consists of a structured program, offering short periods of instruction, experiential exercises done by the couples, and sessions in small groups for open sharing between couples. Leadership is normally provided by a team of two couples who have undergone thorough training.

The third form, which we ourselves started in the Quaker community to which we belong, is usually called the Marriage Enrichment Retreat. It has less structure than any of the others. Leadership is normally by one couple, who have undergone selection and training; the group they lead, which consists of five to eight couples, stays together all the time except for private couple dialogues. The group itself decides the agenda, which is based, therefore, on the needs of the particular couples, and most of the time is devoted to sharing experiences of marriage. This is done mainly through couple dialogues in the presence of the group, which provide a means of mutual learning, encouragement, and support.

The evidence we have suggests that all three patterns of marriage enrichment are highly effective. We have as yet no basis on which to judge whether one form is better than another. It is purely a matter of individual preference. Many leaders, including ourselves, may combine all three patterns in one couples' weekend.

The growth group normally holds its weekly meetings in the informal atmosphere of a home, or the group may move week by week to the homes of all the participating couples. The program normally follows that of one of the weekend patterns, suitably adjusted for sessions widely separated in time.

The general opinion is that the weekend pattern is the more intensive, because it has the advantages of seclusion and continuity. The growth group, however, has the decided advantage that the couples can do "homework" between sessions and report the results back to the group.

There is good reason to believe that groups meeting for a shorter time than the fifteen or sixteen hours or more represented by these programs may not be able to function adequately, since it takes time for inexperienced couples to adjust to these new types of activity and for the group to build up enough trust to make real sharing of experiences possible.

All well-developed marriage enrichment programs use married couples for leadership. Groups of couples differ from groups of individuals, because they are groups of established social units, and it is therefore appropriate for the leadership to come from a similar social unit. The leader couples present very effective models of what the participating couples are being invited to do—to work on their relationship in order to promote growth and enrichment. In all three systems, leader couples are carefully selected and trained.

Follow-up studies of couples who have participated in group experiences show that while real change and growth have been initiated, some couples lose momentum and feel very much the need of continuing help and support. For this reason, most of the experienced agencies are providing "support systems," which are designed to give the couples all possible help to go on working at their marriages and to assist them when they encounter formidable obstacles.

Since marriage enrichment has become more widely known, all sorts of programs have been offered, sometimes by people who don't clearly grasp what is involved. These may be helpful to a limited extent, but they should not be confused with the real thing. Less adequate marriage enrichment programs may be identified as follows: they tend to be of short duration; they are based on talks or lectures incorporating no couple dialogue or interaction; they often feature discussion groups instead of sharing groups; and they are sometimes led by individuals rather than by couples.

Suppose, after all this discussion, you get the idea that you would like to join in a couples' growth group, but you don't know how to begin. You fail to locate any organized marriage enrichment programs in your own community or anywhere within reach. Should you start a group yourself?

Yes, we think you might, by using this book as a basis. Enlist two or three other couples (certainly not more than five or six) who are willing to join you in going through the program in the book. Arrange for them to meet weekly during the six-week period. At the group meetings, simply report to each other your experiences of the unit you have been working on during the past week. This should give you plenty to talk about—you should hold fast to the rule that "we are here, not to exchange opinions, but to share experiences" and to the other rule about allowing no threatening confrontation. Since you will have no professionally qualified leader-couple, let the group pick a couple who seem best able to lead, or take turns at leading.

If you feel that you need a little more support than this, you can get from ACME (see next chapter) a cassette we made called *How to Start a Marriage Enrichment Group*. This gives directions to the group at each stage, so that a leader couple is not necessary. The cassette was prepared for the very purpose of getting a group started in the absence of trained and experienced leadership.

Growth groups provide a highly effective way in which married couples can support, encourage, and learn from each other as they work to build the three essentials into their marriages. There is no doubt that we are about to see, in the near future, an increasingly widespread use of these exciting possibilities.

157

22
Getting into the Marriage Enrichment Movement

What we now call the marriage enrichment movement started in the early 1960s. It has all the characteristics of a truly grass-roots movement, developing spontaneously to meet a need that arose in our culture. A few pioneers got started and then found themselves involved together in a common cause.

We have already referred to the first couples' weekend we led, which was held at Kirkridge, a retreat center in the mountains of eastern Pennsylvania, in October, 1962. But already in January of the same year, Father Gabriel Calvo, the founder of Marriage Encounter, had held his first couples' weekend in Barcelona, Spain. Herbert Otto, a pioneer of the human potential movement, started working with couples' groups at about the same time. Soon after that Leon and Antoinette Smith, of The United Methodist Church, started their Marriage Communication Labs.

Developing from these early beginnings, marriage enrichment grew slowly at first, then at an accelerating pace. It soon joined hands with the new approaches to couple communication started in Minnesota by Sherod Miller and his colleagues; in Pennsylvania, by a team headed by Bernard Guerney, Jr.; and in the national YMCA, by Winifred Coulton of the Family Communication Skills Center in California.

The churches, increasingly concerned about the disturbing rates of family breakdown, gave strong support to the movement. But support came also from the family specialists. Slow at first to recognize the significance of these new developments, they became increasingly involved as they saw this new approach to marriage as a useful supplement to the educational and counseling fields.

In July of 1973, on our fortieth wedding anniversary, and after wide-ranging consultation with others, we established the Association of Couples for Marriage Enrichment (ACME). Our purpose was to create an organization that married couples themselves could join as a way of expressing their support for successful marriage. To our knowledge, no such organization had ever been established before.

We took as ACME's slogan the words "To work for better marriages, beginning with our own." Membership in ACME is open to all couples who will undertake—

1. to support and help each other in seeking growth and enrichment in their own marriages;
2. to promote and support community services effective in fostering successful marriages; and
3. to improve public acceptance and understanding of marriage as a relationship capable of fostering personal growth and mutual fulfillment.

In addition to couple membership, those interested individuals who believe in ACME's goals and want to support the organization may become associate members.

Our hope was that ACME, a citizens' organization with no specific religious affiliation, could include in its ranks all married couples who believed in its objectives, while also coordinating the other national organizations in the field by setting standards and promoting united action. There was no wish or intention to restrict the movement in form or expression; variety was to be encouraged. In this way, we could learn much from each other.

We believed, however, that cooperation would be necessary to give the movement responsible leadership and effective strength.

In three successive years, the leaders of the various national groups have met for consultation. Out of these meetings has emerged the Council of Affiliated Marriage Enrichment Organizations (CAMEO), a loose federation in which all members participate actively, with ACME as coordinator. A list of the present CAMEO organizations is given in Appendix C.

Almost all the marriage enrichment organizations began by providing weekends for married couples, and they continue to do so. It soon became clear, however, that many of the couples who had been through these experiences needed ongoing help and support. Consequently, as we have already explained, we began to design support systems. In ACME these have taken the form of local chapters that organize community programs. Both the National and Worldwide divisions of Marriage Encounter have likewise encouraged the development of local and regional groups which, focused in the parish systems of the churches concerned, seek to support ongoing growth among the "encountered" couples.

Another aspect of these follow-up programs was putting couples to work in promoting the cause of marriage enrichment. Some of those who have experienced considerable growth in their marriages have moved into positions of leadership—not only in leading retreats but also in promoting and organizing the movement. ACME couples have been active in their communities—speaking to PTAs, service organizations, and church groups; organizing public meetings and regional rallies; taking part in press interviews and radio and TV programs; and generally activating the community to be more concerned about marriage and family life. Members of other marriage enrichment organizations have been engaged in similar endeavors. National Marriage Encounter is currently training selected encountered couples to serve as helpers to other couples who, though in trouble, do not need professional counseling.

A long-term goal is social action on behalf of better marriages. ACME has taken the initiative in such actions as proposing that the time is ripe for another White House Conference on the Family (the last was held in 1948); in planning with the Family Service Association of America a project to extend the emphasis of family-serving agencies to include positive-preventive programs and family advocacy; in proposing a reexamination and revision of our procedures in preparation for marriage; and in formulating a plan to extend marriage enrichment to senior citizens.

ACME has also worked out standards for the selection, training, and certification of couple leaders of marriage enrichment events, and these have already been accepted by several of the other national organizations.

As well as its national officers (all are married couples), ACME has representative couples in about forty North American states and provinces. There are ACME member couples in all the American states, in most Canadian provinces, and in about twelve foreign countries.

Marriage Encounter likewise has extended widely across North America and overseas. The Marriage Encounter movement, as already indicated, is divided into two separate groups—Worldwide Marriage Encounter, which tends to be more exclusively Catholic (although it has encouraged "expressions" in other religious groups), and National Marriage Encounter, which welcomes Protestant and Jewish couples to share in its activities.

The best account of the marriage enrichment movement to appear so far is in the book *Marriage and Family Enrichment: New Perspectives and Programs,* by Herbert Otto (see Appendix B). But the movement is so dynamic that some changes have already taken place since its publication.

We would urge all couples who want to support the cause of better marriages to get involved in the marriage enrichment movement by joining one or another of the national organizations. The list in Appendix C includes all organizations known to us that offer couples' retreats and growth groups on a national scale, with the exception of Worldwide Marriage Encounter, which up to now has not united with the others.

For most of our lives, we have worked, to the best of our ability, to promote better marriages. The marriage enrichment movement seems to us to hold out unique promise for the future. We may fittingly conclude our book by quoting something that one of us wrote long years ago, in December, 1947, while crossing the Atlantic on the liner *Queen Elizabeth:*

> We [married couples] have been so furtive and secretive about our married happiness that many people have grown cynical about marriage altogether. It has been said and written that marriage is an overrated and outmoded institution; and the tens of thousands of gloriously happy married people have never raised their voices to deny it. I have been told in all seriousness by an able man and a keen observer of human affairs that he had scarcely ever in his life come in contact with a successful marriage. Why, I said to myself, are the best married people hiding their light under a bushel? Is it not time that some of them emerged from the seclusion of their happy, peaceful homes, and began to "sell" marriage to a generation rapidly becoming cynical and disillusioned about it? (*Marriage Counseling* [London: Churchill, 1948], p. 149)

It took us a long time—from 1947 to 1973, when we established ACME—to find the best way to bring about the hope expressed in these words—the hope that ordinary married couples might themselves take up the cause of better marriages. But the way seems to be opening up at last. The marriage enrichment movement, we are deeply convinced, provides the answer we have long sought. Won't you, who are seeking to find happiness in your own marriage, join us and work with us?

Appendix A

Summary of Work Units

First Week

Saturday: First hour—Evaluation exercise
Second hour—Bargaining session

Sunday to
Friday: Twenty minutes daily—Ten and Ten

Second Week

Saturday: First hour—Marriage potential test
Second hour—Start on growth plan

Sunday to
Friday: Twenty minutes daily—Ten and Ten

Third Week

Saturday: First hour—Evaluation of communication
Second hour—Discussion of Ten and Ten reflections

Sunday to
Friday: Twenty minutes daily—Evaluation of feelings

Fourth Week

Saturday: First hour—Practice communication styles
Second hour—Discuss evaluations of feelings

Sunday to
Friday: Twenty minutes daily—Practice responsive listening

Fifth Week

Saturday: First hour—Exercise on anger
             Second hour—Positive interaction exercise

Sunday to
Friday: Twenty minutes daily—Sharing time

Sixth Week

Saturday: First hour—Exercise on negotiation
             Second hour—Growth plan and contracts

Sunday to
Friday: Twenty minutes daily—Sharing time

Final Evaluation

Suggested two-hour period to review and sum up your total experience with the work units and to complete the evaluation form.

Appendix B

Some Good Books for Further Reading

There is not as yet an extensive literature on marriage enrichment, but books are appearing at an increasing rate. We have selected fourteen from among those known to us, but we do not suggest that this is in any way a comprehensive list. Short descriptions are given for the guidance of the reader. Unfortunately, it is impossible to give prices, because these are constantly changing and are often not stated anywhere in the book.

Bosco, Antoinette. *Marriage Encounter: The Rediscovery of Love.* St. Meinrad, Ind.: Abbey Press, 1972. Written by a professional journalist, this little book describes vividly the origins and early years of the Marriage Encounter as it developed within the Catholic Church and began to become ecumenical. Although the movement has traveled a long way since this was written, no book has since appeared that so adequately and impartially describes it.

Calden, George. *I Count—You Count: The "Do It Ourselves" Marriage Counseling and Enrichment Book.* Niles, Ill.: Argus Communications, 1975. Written by a marriage counselor and ACME member, this is a workbook that leads a couple through a series of exercises designed to develop the spirit of openness and interpersonal communication so essential to a successful marriage.

Clinebell, Charlotte H. *Meet Me in the Middle.* New York: Harper & Row, 1973. An excellent book by a psychotherapist (and ACME member) presenting a new approach to equality between the sexes in terms of interdependence. The application of this approach to the marriage relationship is both practical and inspiring, and the point of view of personal experience from which the book is written is particularly valuable.

Clinebell, Charlotte H., and Clinebell, Howard J., Jr. *The Intimate Marriage.* New York: Harper & Row, 1970. This was one of the earliest books on marriage enrichment, and its intention is to help couples achieve creative intimacy in their relationship. It has been used extensively by couple groups as well as individual couples.

Gordon, Thomas. *Parent Effectiveness Training.* New York: Peter H. Wyden, 1970. This is the basic book, written by a psychologist, that has been widely used across the country to help parents communicate more effectively with their children.

Hauck, Paul, and Kean, Edmund S. *Marriage and the Memo Method.* Philadelphia: Westminster Press, 1975. This little paperback outlines a very practical plan to improve husband-wife communication by writing down thoughts and feelings separately as memos, then exchanging them. This could really help to straighten out some marital misunderstandings.

Keyes, Margaret. *Staying Married.* Millbrae, Cal.: Les Femmes, 1975. This is a most helpful book, full of encouragement and practical ideas for couples ready to work at their marriages. It is written by a marriage counselor who knows her field thoroughly and writes very clearly and convincingly.

Mace, David. *Getting Ready for Marriage.* Nashville: Abingdon, 1972. A practical workbook for couples preparing for marriage that is aimed at enabling couples to examine their relationship in preparation for their life together. Widely used by pastors in premarital counseling.

Mace, David, and Mace, Vera. *We Can Have Better Marriages—If We Really Want Them.* Nashville: Abingdon, 1974. This book explains what marriage enrichment is all about, and it describes the events that led up to the establishment of the Association of Couples for Marriage Enrichment (ACME).

Miller, Sherod, *et al., Alive and Aware: Improving Communications in Relationships.* Minneapolis: Interpersonal Communication Programs, 1975. This is the book that fully describes a widely known program for couple communication training.

Otto, Herbert. *Marriage and Family Enrichment: New Perspectives and Programs.* Nashville: Abingdon, 1976. With twenty-one chapters and contributions from about thirty writers, this book gives the most comprehensive picture available of the marriage enrichment movement, with detailed descriptions of a wide variety of programs and projects.

Powell, John. *The Secret of Staying in Love.* Niles, Ill.: Argus Communications, 1974. This little book is filled with wisdom for married couples that is shared in a highly readable and personal way. The message of the book is that a loving relationship grows out cf effective communication, and the author tells couples how to achieve this.

Satir, Virginia. *Peoplemaking.* Palo Alto, Cal.: Science and Behavior Books, 1972. This widely read book by the well-known consultant in family therapy talks about relationships among family members and shows how they can be improved and enriched.

Smith, Gerald, and Phillips, Alice I. *Me and You and Us.* New York: Peter H. Wyden, 1971. This very practical book for married couples describes forty-seven exercises that the couple can do together to help them understand and improve their relationship. All the experiences have been used and tested out by the author, who is a marriage counselor, and his wife.

Wilke, Richard B. *Tell Me Again, I'm Listening.* Nashville: Abingdon, 1973. A pastoral counselor writes a lively and very readable book about how married couples can get through to each other. The book could be very helpfully used in couple group discussions.

Appendix C

National Marriage Enrichment Organizations in North America

The marriage enrichment movement is developing a variety of programs across North America. Some of these are organized locally, some regionally, some nationally.

This list is confined to those organizations that appear to be providing, *on a national scale,* specific programs in marriage enrichment for married couples. The programs vary somewhat in nature and in scope, but the most common forms are the weekend retreat and the growth group that meets at regular intervals.

We do not consider this list to be complete, and it will obviously have to be expanded in the future. For the time being, we are confining it to a group of organizations that are already in touch with each other and have already sent representatives to national meetings where information has been shared and future policies and plans discussed.

Most of these organizations have expressed a wish to be linked together for ongoing consultation and cooperation in the newly formed Council of Affiliated Marriage Enrichment Organizations (CAMEO), with ACME serving as convener.

Association of Couples for Marriage Enrichment, Inc. (ACME), 459 South Church Street, P. O. Box 10596, Winston-Salem, North Carolina 27108.

Christian Church (Disciples of Christ), Marriage Communication Labs, 222 South Downey Avenue, P. O. Box 1986, Indianapolis, Indiana 46206.

Christian Family Movement, 1655 Jackson Boulevard, Chicago, Illinois 60612.

Church of God, Board of Christian Education, P. O. Box 2458, Anderson, Indiana 46011.

Church of the Brethren, Life Cycle Ministry, 1451 Dundee Avenue, Elgin, Illinois 60120.

Couples Communication Program, Interpersonal Communication Programs, Inc., 2001 Riverside Avenue, Minneapolis, Minnesota 55454.

Family Service Association of America, 44 East Twenty-third Street, New York, New York 10010.

Friends General Conference (Quakers), Marriage Enrichment Task Force, 1520 Race Street, Philadelphia, Pennsylvania 19102.

Institute for the Development of Emotional and Life Skills, Inc. (IDEALS), P. O. Box 391, Pennsylvania State University, University Park, Pennsylvania 16801.

Moravian Church, North, Marriage Enrichment Labs, Board of Educational Ministries, 5 West Market Street, Bethlehem, Pennsylvania 18018.

National Council of Churches, Office of Family Ministries, 475 Riverside Drive, Room 711, New York, New York 10027.

National Marriage Encounter, 955 Lake Drive, St. Paul, Minnesota 55120.

National YMCA, Family Communication Skills Center, 350 Sharon Park Drive, A-23, Menlo Park, California 94025.

Presbyterian Church in Canada, Office of Family Ministries, 50 Wynford Drive, Don Mills, Ontario, M3C 1J7, Canada.

Reformed Church in America, Marriage Enrichment Program, Office of Family Life, Western Regional Center, Orange City, Iowa 51041.

Southern Baptist Convention, Family Ministries Section, 127 Ninth Avenue North, Nashville, Tennessee 37234.

United Church of Canada, National Support Group for Couples Work, 85 St. Clair Avenue, Toronto, Ontario, M4T IM8, Canada.

United Methodist Church, Marriage Communication Labs, Board of Discipleship, P. O. Box 840, Nashville, Tennessee 37202.

United Methodist Church, Marriage Enrichment Program, Board of Discipleship, P. O. Box 840, Nashville, Tennessee 37202.

United Presbyterian Church, National Presbyterian Mariners, 334 North Forty-third Street, Belleville, Illinois 62223.

U.S.A.F. Chaplains Board, Maxwell Air Force Base, Alabama 36112.

U.S. Army Forces Command Chaplain's Office, Headquarters FORSCOM, Fort McPherson, Georgia 30330.

Appendix D

More About the Maces

The authors of books, like writers of plays, usually adopt the practice of keeping modestly in the background. In a book like this, however, in which we inevitably talk a good deal about our own marriage and personally offer a program for other couples to follow, this doesn't seem quite appropriate. We therefore decided to provide a little information about ourselves early in the book, then to offer some further details, for those who might be specially interested, in a concluding appendix.

David was born in Scotland; Vera, in northern England. In 1949, we both came, with our two daughters, to settle in the U.S.A. Here David has spent twenty-one years as a professor—ten years in a theological seminary and eleven years divided between two medical schools. We worked together for a further seven years as joint executive directors of the American Association of Marriage and Family Counselors (1960–67).

In fulfillment of our lifelong commitment to work together for better marriages, we have traveled to some seventy-five countries, initiating programs and projects in sixty-one of them. This has enabled us to study marriage and family life firsthand in all the major human cultures.

Between us, we have been extensively involved in most of the principal organizations serving marriage and the family. In addition to fourteen years spent in building up national marriage counseling services both in Britain and the U.S.A., we were for twelve years consultants in family life to the World Council of Churches in Geneva. David was vice-president of the International Union of Family

Organizations (a consultative body of the United Nations and UNESCO) for four years and chairman of its International Commission on Marriage and Marriage Guidance for fifteen years. He also served terms as president of the National Council on Family Relations and of the Sex Information and Education Council of the U.S. (SIECUS). Both of us have held office in the Groves Conference, a small but influential North American organization of family specialists.

We have written extensively in our field, and books of ours have now been translated into a dozen foreign languages. David has written well over a thousand articles, nearly all about marriage.

We have always seen our own marriage as a partnership of equals, and have from the beginning been committed to growth in our relationship. It took us long years of hard work to achieve really effective communication and to develop a creative approach to conflict. What we have written in this book about the three essentials for a happy marriage comes directly out of our own struggles to achieve a truly creative relationship. We believe we could have been spared years of groping in the dark if we had had access to the knowledge that has now become available as a result of recent research, and which is summarized in this book.

We have lived in Winston-Salem, North Carolina, for ten years and are now senior citizens. One of our daughters lives in Europe, the other in the U.S.A. Both are married and have children.

Appendix E

Evaluation Form

Dear Reader,

We would appreciate your help in evaluating our book. If you are willing to do this, please copy and complete the form below. Your experience in using the book could be very helpful to us when the time comes to revise it, and also, in the planning of future programs in marriage enrichment.

David and Vera Mace

Questionnaire

1. We don't need to know your name, but it would be helpful to have the following information about you. If you are responding as a couple, please check *both* boxes where appropriate.
Sex ( )M ( )F   Age ( ) ( ) Education (check highest level reached): Grade school ( ) ( ) High school ( ) ( ) College ( ) ( ) Graduate school ( ) ( )
Occupations: H_____ W_____
Religion: Catholic ( ) Protestant ( ) Jewish ( ) Other ( )
No preference ( )

2. How did you use the book?
   Skimmed through it ( ) Read it carefully ( ) Carried out the work program ( ) Worked through it with counseling help ( ) Worked through it with a couples' group ( ) Used it as a resource in professional counseling ( )

3. Your overall impression of the book?
   Very helpful ( )   Fairly helpful ( )   Not helpful ( )

4. Did you use the work program?
   Never started ( )   Started but didn't continue ( )   Started and finished ( )

5. Your reaction to the work program?
   Very helpful ( )   Fairly helpful ( )   Not helpful ( )

6. If you would like further information about ACME, check here. ( )

7. Add any specific criticisms or suggestions you may have.

   Please mail your completed form to David and Vera Mace. P. O. Box 5182, Winston-Salem, North Carolina 27103. We regret that we cannot undertake to reply to correspondence, but we would like to carefully read and study your evaluation.